PRAISE FOR *COMPENDIUM*

For those not lucky enough to have been part of
attended Donald Justice's legendary "forms" class,
for everyone to take a seat at the table. What a bles:
classroom once again. Here are the lessons not only of a poet's poet, but of a teacher's
teacher. From the astonishing expressivity of the poetic foot, with its magic ability
to build an entire voice and vision, to the endless nuances of accentual stress, to the
detailed history of such tools—Justice's understanding of prosody was incomparable.
By the time he guides one to the understanding of the architectural movement of a
poem, one has entered the whole cathedral of the medium, step by step. Justice's
brilliant musician's ear, and mastery of the minutest nuances of form, will give any
practitioner—at any stage of their writing—the essential tool-kit. No one who sat in
his presence ever forgot what he taught, or his understanding of what poetry serves. It is
incredible to see it preserved, as in a time capsule, and brought back to us at a moment
when perhaps we need it more than ever. Here is one of the few places one can go for the
uncompromising rigor, finesse and wisdom that are needed to keep this art form alive.

JORIE GRAHAM

Here is a book of prosody that serves not only as a catalogue and history but also, as de-
lineated in David Koehn's meta-prosody introduction and Donald Revell's pithy preface,
the *raison d'etre* for deploying particular metrical and nonmetrical structures. Compiled
from the working course-pack of Donald Justice's poetry classes, *Compendium* is a wide-
ranging encyclopedia of what was and remains possible in the line, word, and syllable.

TYRONE WILLIAMS

This unique and fascinating book—Donald Justice's actual prosody class syllabi, lovingly
preserved by one of his students—offers at once a goldmine of insights from one of our
great thinkers on prosody, and a poignantly revealing time-capsule of American poetics
50 years ago. Justice privileges iambic to the exclusion of other meters, quotes nearly
exclusively from white males, and demonstrates a faith in the power of the Williamsian
free verse line that seems naïve today. But the range of his prosodic conversation across
centuries and his finely-weighted ear for poetry remain perennially vibrant, and the
magnificent, pithy scansion exercises alone are worth the price of the book. Kudos to
editor David Koehn for his devotion and foresight. This book is a must-have for anyone
who wants to understand both the roots of contemporary poetics and those aspects of
the art of poetry that will never go out of date.

ANNIE FINCH

To the art of versification, from chance to traditional methods (which aren't, after all, that
different), both in theory and in practice, Donald Justice brings astonishingly nuanced
insight, not opinion. Compared to some of his more pyrrotechnic contemporaries,
such as Merrill and Hollander, Justice offers incomparable subtlety, austerity, stoicism,
and form as self-effacement. The wealth of quotes and examples from great masters of
prosody, provided without comment, indicate literary erudition at its apex. Here is the
structure of verse in English—the infinite relativity of sounds and silences that compose
the nature of the art.

JAMES GALVIN

COMPENDIUM

COMPENDIUM

A Collection of Thoughts on Prosody
by Donald Justice

Edited by David Koehn & Alan Soldofsky

Cover photo of Donald Justice courtesy of Barbara Hall, 1971

Cover and interior text set in Futura Std and Perpetua Std

Cover and interior design by Gillian Olivia Blythe Hamel

Offset printed in the United States
by Edwards Brothers Malloy, Ann Arbor, Michigan
On 55# Enviro Natural 100% Recycled 100% PCW
Acid Free Archival Quality FSC Certified Paper

Library of Congress Cataloging-in-Publication Data

Names: Justice, Donald, 1925-2004 author. | Koehn, David editor. | Soldofsky,
    Alan editor.
Title: Compendium : a collection of thoughts on prosody / by Donald Justice ;
    edited by David Koehn & Alan Soldofsky.
Description: Oakland, California : Omnidawn Publishing, 2017. | Includes
    bibliographical references and index.
Identifiers: LCCN 2016045485 | ISBN 9781632430328 (pbk. : alk. paper)
Subjects: LCSH: English language--Versification. | Poetics.
Classification: LCC PE1505 .J85 2017 | DDC 808.1--dc23
LC record available at https://lccn.loc.gov/2016045485

Published by Omnidawn Publishing, Oakland, California
www.omnidawn.com (510) 237-5472 (800) 792-4957
10 9 8 7 6 5 4 3 2 1
ISBN: 978-1-63243-032-8

TABLE OF CONTENTS

I have ported the hard copy packet of Donald Justice's prosody course syllabus around with me since I was but a young adjunct professor and an aspiring writer who was probably more talk than walk. The edges are now frayed, the paper yellowed, coffee-cup stained, and wrinkled. I had the good fortune of taking the course at The University of Florida the final time it was offered, and so likely have the benefit of seeing the course packet in its most refined and complete form. I have one of the last full stacks, save for one page which my friend and classmate Scott Brennan was able to fill in from his own incomplete version. Justice's class at The University of Florida changed the course of my life.

As a student, I recall spending time in class contemplating the duration of a syllable in the mouth of Justice. I would listen and watch the second hand of the classroom's clock seem to pause. In the pause, in the consideration of the syllable, revelations unbound by time and as primal as the sexual urge lit up my senses. A friend once described the attention to prosody as a trick to keep the editorial side of the mind at bay so that the unbridled imagination could reign.

I still find this sleight-of-hand true when reading and even more true when writing. During this period of my growth, words came into sharper focus, and lines started to illuminate with the colors of the palette of prosody. For decades, the scope and rewards of Donald's insight continued to unfold for me, my ear became increasingly musical, and this attention to sound seemed to intensify all of my faculties.

Now, I have the good fortune of bringing *Compendium* forward. Part textbook, part history project, *Compendium* brings Donald Justice's original prosody syllabus and student exercise packet to our community. Though I have appreciated poetry all my adult life as both a reader and a writer, and though I revisit the ideas my mentors have passed on to me, I never thought the responsibility of being the steward of this remarkable text would—or even should—fall on me.

On one hand, I ask myself, "Who am I to do so?" And yet, in the absence of any other alternative, I feel compelled to wade into territory that I fear far exceeds my depth. Through the lens of time that spans from early tutelage by our mentors to their deaths and toward our own horizon, memory and responsibility establish a presence that overshadows insecurity. The pastiche of recollection takes on a shape and a form. A friend reminds me of Justice's introduction to Weldon Kees, where Justice claims no special knowledge of Kees and provides a preface only for the privilege of calling him forward to a new set of readers. While Justice's knowledge of Kees was deeper than he would give himself credit for, I take comfort that Justice felt it quite natural to shepherd readers toward great work that lacked popular favor.

The Collage Process

I've had decades to engage with *Compendium*. Yet, my grasp is partial at best. One of the many powerful dimensions of Justice's text is that it is open to many modes of reading. The collage process Justice employed to present his instructional materials possesses a composer's quality. The structure of which possesses a unique beauty. His insights serve as a sort of de facto taxonomy, an organically designed system that he uses to present his lecture on each respective aspect of the evolution of poetic form. The collage, the aggregation, creates an anaphora with variable refrain.

The selection, the choices accumulate to present a point of view filtered through the point and counterpoint of quotations from prosody's most astute minds. To show how syllabics evolved into accentual-syllabics, he provides us with a line from Hopkins to capture perhaps the first instance of sprung rhythm in the English language. We experience a sense of one poet standing on the shoulders of another until a breakthrough is made, a new invention made, allowing the endeavor to push forward. Only here and there does Justice insert his own prose, his own voice, his own text into this collage, this amalgamation of learning. This spareness of approach belies a kind of baseline assumption, a sort of take it as you will—use or don't use as you see fit. He presents his findings, but he does not extend the bias of his personal tastes.

This is ultimately the beauty of the syllabus and the purpose of preserving it, leaving it in large part as it was originally presented to me. I see surprise after surprise, as each layer discloses to the neophyte and to the expert more than enough to consider in a quick 15 minute gloss or enough grist for a lifetime. As one explores the text, one can reflect upon a few quotes on the subject of a topic of prosody and then move on, never the worse for having done so. A cursory review will deliver gems like this one from IA Richards:

This texture of expectations, satisfactions, disappointments, surprises, which the sequence of syllables brings about, is rhythm. And the sound of words comes to its full power only through rhythm. Evidently there can be no surprise and no disappointment unless there is expectation and most rhythms perhaps are made up as much of disappointments and postponements and surprises and betrayals as of simple, straightforward satisfactions. Hence the rapidity with which too simple rhythms, those which are too easily 'seen through,' grow cloying or insipid unless hypnotical states intervene, as with much primitive music and dancing and often with metre.

Or the reader might take one topic of the taxonomy, looking at the sequence of the various quotes and examples, and begin to recognize layers of connection. Each new encounter with the text reveals more stimulating discoveries. Or, correspondingly, look at one throughline across the text. As proxy, consider the throughline of Yvor Winters quotes from the excerpt in the Syllabics section to the Accentual Syllabics section to the Sound and Sense section to the Free Verse section, including a cool little section showing Winters' scan of Williams' "To Waken an Old Lady." Such throughlines argue for their own fascinations of history and aesthetics. Use the index we have added to *Compendium* as a tool to construct such throughways.

Simply, perusing the text leads to pleasure. Consider trying to write a song like Cole Porter as selected by Justice. Chase down the syllabics variations in the examples provided by Justice from Marianne Moore. The text reveals its value in an idiosyncratic but ultimately harmonious way.

Relevance to the Contemporary

Often, the contemporary values the civic over depth because in large part the writers of our time don't know what they don't know. The anachronistic affections the contemporary might have for Niedecker, Ginsberg, or Dove reside in the politics of content, though their popularity is also evidence of these writers' mastery and application of the impactful subtleties of prosody. Prosody is the litmus test of the genius of the art. Prosody is the very medium of the poet's domain, and its mis-application reveals the shallowness of the poetry and the poet. The lack of awareness of previous invention corresponds to a subsequent inability to do anything new.

Prosody has inhabited every culture's poetic traditions and sensibilities. In fact the "content" of first century B.C. Chinese poetry, the shi form, had no value absent the required prosody. This is nowhere more evident than in the kaleidoscopic view of Weinberger and Paz in their "19 ways of Looking at Wang Wei." Yes, this slim volume illustrates the problems of translation—but the very heart of the heart of the problem is that shi prosody is not translatable. That is the application of craft—the aesthetic depth of the artist is not commutable.

In some ways, I face a similar challenge here. Justice's taxonomy attempts to render, in our native English, what can be translated to us: its genetic markers for invention and growth. Such genetic markers of course exist in Chinese, in Russian, in Italian, in all modern languages, and in the dead languages like Latin, too, but Justice took it upon himself to preserve unique movements.

The reason this compendium matters is that the collage of materials tells a story in which the narrator is absent. I want to provide access to the riches but cannot give away all its secrets—the magic of the experience of having studied this material with Justice himself. As a teacher, Justice opened the door to the mansion, showed you the thread to pull to unravel the tapestry, sketched the outline, and knew that was enough for the interested to pursue to the completed picture. Now Donald is absent, but this text remains. That is why I feel it is all the more important to faithfully bring this text forward, so that the integrity at the core of his discoveries can live on in the world.

I make no claim to be an expert on Justice's poetry or the study of prosody, and I anticipate with much excitement that there will be droves of his former students who will share their stories and experiences of this course and their time with Justice. You'll hear the very accurate explanation of Justice as wildly experimental—and in no way a poet who adheres strictly to traditional poetic forms in the broadest sense of the word. Justice saw prosody as a set of nomenclatures for poet-composers to use in making their music. Justice sought spontaneity of form—though a spontaneity informed by its relationship to poetic traditions in the English language. This belies his upbringing as a musician and his abrupt attempts at writing concertos and, most notably, his deep affection for John Cage and the use of chance in poetry.

Structure & Chance

Part of the structure of Justice's prosody seems particularly informed by his investigation of chance. Everyone who knew Donald knew his affection for poker and, more broadly, for gambling. But he also knew the odds of these games, and the logical, mathematical part of his analytical mind seemed drawn to the intersection of music and chance and art and poetry. There is no formal thesis here, but rather a kind of scrapbook that has a broader motive. Just one gloss end-to-end will leave readers uncertain of what they have just read—but also hungry to return and better understand their reading. Even those who don't return will be left fundamentally changed because, as Nabokov says, "Find What the Sailor Has Hidden—that the finder cannot unsee once it has been seen." The material possesses no hidden secrets; the treasures lie in plain sight and simply need be discerned to open the artist's mind to their possibilities. I'd hope that in any reading of this reclaimed text, these would be the stakes, the chance the reader takes.

The order of topics in *Compendium* reflects Justice's historical and aesthetic point of view. In his "Summary of Types" he asserts the evolution of how the art has chosen to "count" sound. The act of counting for Justice is the mathematical relationship of music to sound. To overcomplicate prosody in Justice's world is to not understand it well enough. The summary proposes that we started by counting syllables and, closely thereafter, stressed or accented sound. We then started composing in lines where we regulated syllables and stresses. These regular patterns established the baseline against which greater and greater variations have been built—free verse, but an attenuated and natural evolution of this variation.

Silence & the Open Field

Justice's "George Elliston Poetry Foundation Lecture, 1967: No. 9. Donald Justice: 'Silence & the Open Field: John Cage and Charles Olson'" begins with a quote from Cage, "If there are rules who made them?" The illustration here thwarts the very study Justice aspired to uncover in his own study of "sound and the spaces between" or prosody. How were the rules of prosody arrived at? The "open field" of the space between the "unintended" and the "intended" represents the opportunity of the contemporary to inform practice with the very nature of the everyday: its ordinariness and its randomness. The bevel of "chance" that Justice uses when discussing Cage (and, in contrast, Olson's "Projective Verse") provides the best available exposition of Justice's appeal to the act of collage, or the act of compiling in a composition the postmodern notions of fragmentation and deconstruction of perspective.

Justice seems to want to evade "conscious control" but does not need evidence of this loss in the poem itself, as "form is content is continuity." The full lecture is filled with terms that call out to this evasion of control: discontinuity, coin toss, chance, dissimilars, mixtures, randomness, indeterminacy, disjointed, conversions, referential, multiplicity, freewheeling, improvisation, fragments, sample, unplanned, junctures, confused, chance operations, asymmetrical, non-intention, inclusive, open, mixture, bursts, bit-by-bit, and "a pair of socks." This evasiveness seems almost pathological, the result a kind of curation of fragmentariness at the very heart of Compendium.

Why include this at all? I include an excerpt from this lecture because the selection informs the reader both of the wildness of Justice's mind for experimentation and his affection for the artfulness of the odds, of chance, of coincidence. These are concepts that will serve the reader of Compendium well. Reading Compendium through this lens opens the reader to introducing these ideas into their own work with a level of freedom one might describe as arbitrary. So, to me, if as Cage suggests, "composition is the organization of sound," then reading a fragmentary text about the techniques of rhythm for poetry makes sense.

The Summary of Types

The Summary of Types section is the entire course on prosody distilled. The model Justice establishes in this section of commentary on the subject by others is one consistently applied throughout. Justice almost never inserts his personal opinion into the text. The argument, the point of view, is suggested or implied through the sampling. The course is framed, not accidentally, in chronological order from Coleridge (1800), to Wordsworth (1817), I.A. Richards (1924), Yvor Winters (1930), and J.V. Cunningham (1960). And then he stops, as if to note that the contemporary is in flight…and the framing of prosody in the contemporary is now up to us…

In later sections the sampling of commentary is followed by a series of examples of poets and sections of poems illustrating both the prosodic idea and usually the acceptable exception to the prosodic rule or idea—and in some cases the outlier or limit of the prosodic idea.

And the examples are not, as they might first appear, haphazard. They represent various ages of the art, various strategies for employing the form of prosody in discussion, and an aesthetic argument of how prosody informs the depth of an artist and differentiates the artist gifted in prosody from one who isn't. I suspect Justice might protest this last point—he might opine in this day and age that no poet is obligated to learn prosody and that we should only do so out of interest in the history of the art. He might argue that the study here is for historical purposes only and that no poet let alone any reader needs to bother with prosody if they don't want to—it is an alternative way of thinking about the art that no one need feel obliged to consider. And yet, "thoughts against thoughts in groans grind."

In this "dance of words" we know dancing is fun, anyone can dance, and no formal training is required to dance beautifully or to dance joyously, yet we know that dancing in its highest form is choreographed, sometimes (as in Kabuki) down to the smallest of movements. Such is the relationship of prosody to poetry.

The Syllabics Section

In the Syllabics section Justice privileges simplicity and highlights commentary from Cunningham and Winters. Syllabics affords a poem the language of the everyday, an ease of pressure on the force of language demanded by accentual verse. Justice's focus on syllabics in his own work is largely known. His synthesis of the French surrealists and his application of syllabics was an individual artistic decision. For example, the deceptive simplicity of his book of poems, *Night Light*, assumes these principles. Justice's examples, from Elizabeth Daryush to Lorca to Melville, don't betray this allegiance. Perhaps in the examples from Plath or Tate we also see an inkling of it, but barely and sparely.

The samples from Tate and Plath highlight for me the reinforcing principle that many contemporary writers consider them to be poets of lesser craft orientation. Yet once we open the Pandora's box of prosody and look closely at Plath, we see that the well is bottomless and may take us all the way to Sappho. And with Tate, one's pursuit of his application of prosody is boundless and ever fruitful—with Tate syllabics in particular is a valuable wedge into his depth.

The Accentuals Section

While accentual verse, with deep roots in the Germanic origins of English, would suggest we can easily apply it, generally the application of syllabics is considered "easier." And yet, broadly speaking, rap and spoken word in the contemporary often unwittingly seem to take advantage of the accentual form—despite the contemporary ear's inability to hear it. Hopkins' take on what he called "Sprung Rhythm" is "the most natural of things." And we see, across the contemporary, versifiers teaching children's verse as exemplary of this prosodic element. The roots of this attempt to teach accentual this way come from Justice and his mini-lesson in the accentual section called Dipodic Verse. The next time you see a lesson highlighting accentual meter via children's verse, and using "Peas porridge hot" in particular—you can now source the origin.

The Accentual-Syllabics Section

Ultimately Justice orients the learner to the section on Accentual-Syllabics by covering Syllabic and Accentual verse. Justice would likely argue covering Syllabics and then Accentuals is largely an arbitrary decision—a decision likely made to make it easy for a student to start counting syllables before they meet the struggle of counting and understanding accent. Even this pattern of walking the poet from syllabics into accentuals is a Wintersian trait that Justice perpetuates. What do I mean by Wintersian? This is a question worth considering now because the commentary in the Accentual Syllabics section is started with a long passage from Yvor Winters, beginning "I must now summarize my position in general terms…" which you can very easily, and probably rightly, take as the foundation—at least in contraposto—for Justice's position.

Winters framed the basis from which all alignments to and reactions from Prosody have been formed. His students make up a pantheon of the contemporary and they include Donald Revell, Thom Gunn, Donald Hall, Robert Pinsky, and Robert Hass. He was also a mentor to J.V. Cunningham and Bunichi Kagawa—and to Donald Justice.

And so, in the text, we get our first imposition from Justice. Here in Accentual Syllabics he feels compelled to clear things up. We hear Justice quietly complain that he must reluctantly taxonify the "so-called 'permissive variations.'" I read into Justice's reluctance to impose on the poet's discernment a direct reaction to Winters' desire to impose. And what is lovely in his way is that Justice was inclined to illustrate how a poem says something—how Frost or Keats or Stevens or even Dickinson might be read—decisively one way, say as a poem of iambic tetrameter with permissive variations, and then deconstruct that entire reading, asserting decisively that poem is really anapestic trimeter with permissive variations. I think Justice felt his classification of permissive variations was exact. If one was working in Accentual Syllabics these were the limits of acceptable variability, and if you pushed outside these you were doing something other than writing in accentual-syllabics.

This is also a good time to note that Justice did not include the traditional meters or the standard feet in his syllabus on prosody. He assumed your knowledge of these things but made no assumptions about your ability to apply that knowledge. He wanted the poet to hear in the everyday these traditional meters and find places where they elide. I remember he assigned the class an exercise to listen to our own conversations throughout the day—to listen for iambic pentameter that existed in the colloquial. I brought to discussion the phrase "Why don't you use American Express?" and an hour-long discussion ensued about the imprecision of the content, its metrical basis, and the musicality of the phrase irrespective of standard written English.

Here Justice showed the strict rules of the permissible variations (the pressure on the form that perhaps initiates evolution in prosody), and that which falls completely outside the form's parameters—a mistake in form, a faltering or an inability to achieve its rigor in a natural and artistic manner.

Justice's knowledge of traditional feet and meters as well as alternative and extended feet and meters was comprehensive, but he had no tolerance for the expert's approach. The backbone of his understanding of versification surfaces in this commentary section. McAuley's *Versification* is the *Strunk and White* of prosody, and at a slim 80 pages in its second printing one can see how many of the comments on Accentual Syllabics Justice pulls from this singular, universe-defining book. That said, the boutique doctoral view of the world, the paeons, epitrites, cretics and even the molossus played little if at all into his point of view. The esoterica of prosody was not the concern of Justice. Music was his concern.

Sound & Sense

In the section Sound and Sense, we see Justice emerging like an oboe in the concert chamber of the orchestra of commentary in the text. In sections 7 and 8 his voice rises above the discussion with a clarion call of:

> rhythm is not only one of the significant means by which special attention is called to the words of a poem...but for its own sake as well. And all this true, more or less, whether the poem is written in the traditional meters or in free verse, whether the 'music' of the poem approaches the one extreme of song or the other extreme of speech.

We also see Justice moving beyond a Wintersian point of view, and into an acceptance of the point of view that the necessity of prosody can be argued away. There is good reason to debunk all the reasons one might discard prosody to the trash bin of history. He even accelerates the argument that the din of free verse lends itself to the musicality that the traditional meters lay claim. For:

> if the meters do represent or imitate anything in general, it may be of nothing more (or less) than some psychological compulsion, a sort of counting on the fingers or stepping on the cracks, magic to keep an unpredictable world under control.

And yet…

The Song Section

In the section on Song, Justice himself a composer, defers almost entirely to Auden. Justice's attention to Song can't be downplayed. And I think a primary challenge here is to look at the sample "Sing, cuccu…" as even folks like myself with the most basic of musical training can sing this song based on the notation provided. I think the most amazing dimension of this exercise is that we can all sing it according to the beats in the notation and we will all sound similar in rhythm but our tone and the key we sing in will differ and yet we are all singing the same song. Somewhere in this harmonization, prosody's value to the imagination lingers.

The Free Verse Section

The story for the poet at this point in the text is in its denouement. At this point the poet should have the realization that free verse emerged from a set of historical and practical contexts in direct relation to the use of accentuals with its Germanic roots and syllabics with latinate roots. Within the free verse section Justice classifies short line and long line free verse. He further sub-classifies both types both for organizational and for historical purposes. Long line free verse is classified as type A, "oracular," and type B, the "loosened blank verse line," and type C, "prose broken into lines." Short line is summarized as type A, the "imagist" line, and type B as "short lines with a syllabic source." This tidy classification system is worth mentioning because it applies so well and so thoroughly to the contemporary.

In some modes of the contemporary there is a tendency to subscribe to one or several of these types and to mix and match—all of which Justice would consider healthy. I'll also add that the spectrum of Prose Poem to the L A N G U A G E poem equally fits within his prosody. In both cases there is a particular religion about their content, but in Justice's view their music (or lack thereof) or rhythm (or lack thereof) "is not only one of the significant means by which special attention is called to the words of a poem…but for its own sake as well." There is no discord between prosody and experimentation—in all cases prosody simply informs the experiment if the poet chooses to take advantage of the medium. As a painter may or may not choose to use a paintbrush, knowing its techniques can only more effectively inform the painter of how to not use the paintbrush.

Addenda & Bibliography

The addenda, the bibliography, the exams are resources for the diligent to explore. The section on Quantitative verse in particular. My own fascination with Catullus began with a challenge to write hendecasyllabic verse without the mishap of falling into iambic pentameter or even worse misshapen and mistaken iambic pentameter. Now in my case this small sampling, this tease, led me away to a lifetime of working on translations of Catullus. I can only hope others tap into the unlimited reservoirs of resource, history, and imagination linked to this text.

Publisher Ambivalence

Before I published my first book, I passed the idea of this project around to many publishers, but none were interested. I also shared the project idea with other poets, and though many thought the project worthy, nobody really took it seriously. However, as my own writing began to pick up traction, winning a book award and receiving some favorable reviews, I suddenly found publishers eager to take on the project. I now had the ability to promote Justice's legacy, and so the prospect of bringing this project to reality was given new life.

After considering several publishers, I ultimately felt Omnidawn Publishing would be the best home for the project, as I had taught from this packet's curriculum for their fundraisers several times in the past, and I felt confident they shared a passion for the material. I also saw this book as way to be part of Omnidawn's growing family and to bring to Omnidawn a deeply investigative book of poetics, in the manner of their past publications. The editors understand my long-term connection to Donald, appreciate his influence on my work, and respect my goal of developing more than simply a new textbook on prosody; I wanted a means to re-invigorate contemporary aesthetics with a depth that Donald's nuanced understanding of prosody provides.

As much as I have attempted to preserve the integrity of the original, there are several modifications that had to be applied. The judgements we made to make the text viable were few, but notable. The first compromise we made was on the length of the original excerpts chosen by Justice. In some instances, we shortened Justice's selections so that they included no more than 49% of the original poem. In this way we could preserve the specificity of Justice's original examples without violating copyright laws.

We also found the reproduction of the courier typewriter font Justice used (and that added such a distinctive visual element to the syllabus) impractical. These pages were occasionally annotated in his own handwriting to correct notes he saw with his typing or the typewriter's layout of a section. Certainly part of the charm of the original syllabus, the production quality of the book by Omnidawn, does justice to Justice even if we can't reproduce the unique personal quality of his original typewritten and revised pages.

Workbook Modules.

To accommodate creative writing teachers who need exercises on prosody more accessible to younger students, we also provide supplementary material to augment Justice's original document. This workbook is available to all who purchase *Compendium*. At the end of this text, we provide access information to the modules at the Omnidawn website. For every topic in Justice's taxonomy in *Compendium* there is an accompanying module. These modules use contemporary examples—most written since Justice last taught. Furthermore, these modules, developed by Alan Soldofsky with his undergraduate students, are specifically designed to be used in conjunction with the Justice text. Alan's work with his students at San Jose State University has validated the utility of the text and the exercises for MFA students and undergraduates alike. Justice, as an instructor, would place the examples in *Compendium* in modules like these, verbally of course, in class. The modules created for Alan's students replicate the spirit of Donald's work as a teacher— the lesson plans or framework for instruction, so to speak.

Gratitudes

I'd be remiss if I failed to express my infinite gratitude to William Logan and to the recently departed Jean Justice who worked through William to empower me to take this project to completion. Further, I was blessed to have the support of Alan Soldofsky in developing the modules adjacent to the core text. Lastly there is a long list of people whom I could not have completed this project without, including Rusty Morrison, Scott Brennan, Peter Burghardt, Sharon Zetter, and Linda Bergamo.

I have to explicitly thank Rusty Morrison who let me use *Compendium* by Donald Justice for several years as the base text for the "Omnidawn Online Poetry Workshop: Prosody as a Revision Strategy." This experience validated that practicing poets could and would find lasting value in Justice's approach to prosody. The featured guest poets and the attending poets who participated in the "Omnidawn Online Poetry Workshop: Prosody as a Revision Strategy" were hugely valuable in helping me think through how to frame this text. The featured guest poets included: William Logan, Jim Daniels, Maxine Chernoff,

Gillian Conoley, Brian Teare, Arthur Sze, Tyrone Williams, Robert Hass, Rusty Morrison, Norma Cole, Craig Santos Perez, Matthew Zapruder, Sherwin Bitsui, Cody Walker, and Donald Revell.

Lastly, I cannot say enough about Donald Revell who not only participated in these online workshops, but as a Wintersian (a student of Yvor Winters), like Donald Justice, found it in his immense heart to write a preface that establishes the imaginative, rhetorical, logical and ultimately magical framework for the book.

David Koehn
Berkeley, California

PREFACE

In both sacred and secular writings we may receive, at any
instant, a sense of things inaccessible suddenly made accessible,
where grammar and desire are miraculously at one.

— Geoffrey Hill, "The Weight of the Word"

Like prayer, prosody is both a form and an energy, a compulsion to compel
the Word in words. And like prayer, it retains its original necessity in living
breath: one by one and by one. So does singularity address the universal, only
to reach more deeply inward, finding instruction there via absolutes. In form
of speech is change, yes; but only in the form of change does our speech take
shape. Exactly here, desire enters in, shaping grammars, patterns, emphases
and durations into poems first imagined as themselves, kindling that very
desire. The rhythms are forever personal, albeit they begin and end, like breath
itself, in a common place and in convention. Desire launched the thousand
ships, each of which adventured on its own and each of which was a perfect
emblem of the others. There is only one emotion: all of them. There is only one
prosody: the sum of passions fixed upon the syllables as and how they move.
That Geoffrey Hill describes this unity as miraculous simply underscores the
supernatural power of convention to distinguish clearly all that it unites in
clarity. This is the power and province of the teacher, of the prosodist, of the
eclectic summa speaking in a common space.

There are precedents. Prosodies are rational, and the nearest will
always be the most provocative, adumbrating entire canons of poetry with
bold strokes of Idea and with the legerdemain of unspoken Ideality. In 1602,
Thomas Campion's insistence upon quantitative meters ("the facility and
popularity of rhyme creates as many poets as a hot summer flies") may well
have provoked Samuel Daniel to write *A Defense of Rhyme* ("our rhyme doth add
more grace and hath more of delight than ever bare numbers"), but now, at the
quiet distance of four centuries, Campion and Daniel consort well together
in hushed appendices worldwide. Yet nearer our own time, the adumbrations

necessary to the useful assertion of a rational prosody chafe and jar. I look at
my oldest copy of Ezra Pound's *ABC of Reading* and I find the margins full of
expletives and exclamation marks scored by a hot hand—mine. I mind how
I puzzled over and protested against the objectivist anonymities and overlays
of Louis Zukofsky's *A Test of Poetry*. And to this day, I feel real pain of remorse
when I recall the look on the face of my graduate professor of prosody—Elias
Schwartz, the most gentle of scholars, and surely the finest exegete of Yvor
Winters' poetics—as I told him I meant to do my term paper on Olson's
Human Universe: a proposal in every way antagonistic to Winters' *Quest for
Reality*. Every battle of books interleaves humane juxtapositions. Pound was
entirely correct to avow that, in a poem, "syllables juxtapose in beauty." And
there we have both the how and the why of prosody, from Bion to Bunting, from
scop to slam. There, too, we have the fixed points in a swirling controversy.
Juxtaposition is technique, the living hand upon the syllables. And as to beauty,
it is an Ideality with never the same name twice. There needs, as Hill implies,
a miracle. There needs what Sir Philip Sidney calls a "moving."

> For who will be taught, if he be not moved with desire to be
> taught? And what so much good doth the teaching bring forth…
> as that it moveth one to do that which it doth teach? For, as
> Aristotle saith, it is not *gnosis* but *praxis* must be the fruit; and
> how *praxis* can be, without being moved to practise; it is no hard
> matter to consider.

> – from "The Defence of Poetry"

Motive and miracle prove to be one and the same actuality. Its name is Teacher
and its eclectic summa shows the jagged matter of prosody in distinctive
motion moving. Via the teacher, praxis and gnosis become accessible, each to
each. The grammars of desire sanctify the secular ground of making poems in
company with one's particular generation. Donald Justice was, is a poet who
brought generations of younger women and men to such a ground, there to
place their hands upon the syllables moving. His *Prosody*, evinced in the same
ether as Pound's *ABC*, Winters' *Quest*, and Zukofsky's *Test*, moves the reader
to practice a sure sense of the miraculous newly received upon the basis of
one singular knowledge, duly evinced. Here is a compelling universal, freshly
imagined as itself.

Donald Revell
Las Vegas, Nevada

COMPENDIUM

FROM "SILENCE AND THE OPEN FIELD: JOHN CAGE AND CHARLES OLSON"

The lectures collected in the book *Silence*, from which most of you will recognize that I am drawing very extensively, were themselves given out of the need for poetry, Cage says. It seemed to me possible that given this concern for poetry and while granting that what Cage has said has been most directly relevant to music—though not without its asides concerning dance, painting, Oriental lore, mushrooms, and so on—a very wide range of interests—we might still see what application to poetry his ideas could have. And of course, in procuring this talk, taking a first cue from Cage, I consulted the Book of Changes. By using the coin oracle, I arrived at the hexagram called, "The arousing shock: thunder," which in turn led to the one called, "The corners of the mouth: providing nourishment". The result of the chance operation seemed too appropriate to pass over. For the hexagram "The arousing"— you know the Book of Changes? Anyway—of that particular hexagram, the commentaries include these observations. "Shock brings success. Shock comes—oh oh. Laughing words—ha ha. The shock terrifies for a hundred miles and he does not let fall the sacrificial spoon and chalice. Thus, in fear and trembling, the superior man sets his life in order and examines himself." And of "The corners of the mouth," the other hexagram I came up with, "starting with the mouth through which we take food for nourishment, the thought leads to nourishment itself." Feeling that I'd hit upon the right and propitious signs for John Cage then I took heart.

In the lecture on nothing, Cage says, "Our poetry now is the realization that we possess nothing. Anything, therefore, is a delight." Poetry may be anywhere like music. If composition is the organization of sound, it includes, of course, musical tones. It may also include, once silence is allowed to enter, noise. As in modern architecture, especially in its use of glass, music is left free to include the environment, what's happening, what is. Is such a thing possible in poetry? I don't know. One of the prime difficulties in following the direction of Cage's thought and applying it to poetry is the difficulty of making the proper conversions and translations of terms from one art to another, if that's possible at all, or if it's necessary. Some features are immediately clear, however. For one, what I'm tempted to call the naturalistic bent or bias of a theory, in this sense at least, that the art with which Cage is concerned seems to point back toward life and life in nature, almost to seek to eradicate any distinction we might wish to make between art and nature, and in a much more radical way than any of the poets we've observed in previous lectures leaning in that direction. If this word music is sacred, says Cage, quite early, we can substitute a more meaningful term: organization of sound. Let's read poetry here for music. Or we could read art there: organization of something. Once the sense of its being in some way sacred is dropped, new possibilities regarding the work become available, as, for instance, they can be natural: a representation of how things are. What, asks Cage, is more angry than the flash of lightning and the sound of thunder? The attitude is, finally, one of affirmation. An affirmation of life. Though with this difference from some other sorts of affirmation, some of our American sorts, more Eastern, I imagine. That it is so because it doesn't constitute an attempt to bring order out of chaos nor to suggest improvements in creation but is simply a way of waking up to the very life you're living, which is so excellent once one lets it act of its own accord. To arrive at this condition, one gets one's mind and one's desires out of its way.

This point, the obligation to clear oneself from the field, to stop interfering, which stems, as I suggest, from an affirmative preference, simply stated, for life over art leads to a concern with a method or methods that will permit art, so to speak, to happen. And here in particular, it seems to me, Cage is writing about music, all through suggestions for poetry which haven't been, to my knowledge, really tried out. We're not interested in any of the rather superficial attempts to make comparisons between, say, the rhythms of music and the rhythms of poetry, which have been tried in the past, as in the attempt by Sidney Lanier, the flutist, to impose a musical time interpretation of poetic meters on what had been written according to other prescriptions, nor with any attempt to say that such and such a feature of verse, the somewhat indeterminate rise and fall of pitch, for instance, is like the melody of conventional music, nor with calling the reversal of several metrical feet in a row a kind of counterpointing, as Hopkins did. No. We'll not try to convert or compare the terms so exactly, for such conversions remain figurative. We'll try to speak as practically as we can.

Without becoming too technical or too detailed, let me try to review some of the compositional methods Cage has described for music, keeping in mind their possible applications to poetry. Some, of course, involve chance operations. The Book of Changes provides for obtaining of oracles by the tossing of coins. And the results may be used to determine the materials of the work and their disposition. And the process is complicated. It's fun, though.

And it involves a good deal of ingenuity in the drawing up of charts, the nature of which needn't detain us here, since we're not concerned with the method as strictly a musical method, but as a method of working with poetry, potentially. In the nature of the charts, the writer would have to devise for that would, since different materials would be employed having different characteristics, necessarily be different too. Another method involves using imperfections of the actual paper on which the writing is to be done as a sort of chart or guide to compose it, or a writer, as the case might be. There are other methods, but these two should be adequate to suggest one range of extending possibility. In both cases, the method remains a mean of exercising control over some areas of the word. What may be significant is that this control is not conscious, as we would ordinarily think of conscious control. The means seems mechanical, arbitrary, but with paradoxical implications in the result.

For if, as Cage suggests in a slightly different connection, if we reach the point where the ego no longer blocks action, if the self has been cleared from the field, then, as he adds, a fluency obtains which is characteristic of nature itself. With so much under control, a new kind of freedom not intimately involved with the individual ego, as we normally think freedom to be, becomes possible. Thus becomes possible to make, Cage says, a musical composition, but we might substitute poetry here or simply the word "something": a something, the continuity of which is free of individual taste and memory, psychology, and also as the literature and traditions of the art. The procedure strikes me as analogous, in some ways, to the playing of a game, a game which is both fun and serious, abstracted from life but resembling it—again, paradoxically— in ways different from those of which works produced in accordance to any of the old imitation theories are capable. The freedom as it invites the inside out—goodbye ego—invites the outside in. Welcome the environment, the world. And in this sense is inclusive rather than exclusive. There's room for any kind of event, for all events.

Henry Moore, whom I've quoted before, remarks that, "a large piece of stone or wood placed almost anywhere at random in a field, orchard, or garden, immediately looks right or inspiring." Or as Cage, going further, puts it, "the idea of relations being absent, anything may happen," adding, "a mistake is beside the point, for once anything happens, it authentically is." Values, as we're used to speaking of them, reside in the conventional made-up world of art, not in this world of art which so resembles life.

Now it seems to me perfectly clear that poetry too might be composed according to such procedures. We've seen already in previous lectures various instances of attempts to evade conscious control as well as of attempts to organize disparate and unusual bodies of material, usually in a search for the new out of some weariness for the conventional productions of high art.

But, as I said, the difficulty in applying Cageian methods to poetry, which seem to line a proper conversion of terms from one field to another—I have no formula for doing this; only a suggestion that it may be done. Yet some clues can be drawn from Cage's definitions. He writes, "structure in music is its divisibility into successive parts, from phrases to long sections. Form is content, the continuity," elsewhere saying, "the expressive content, the morphology of continuity." "Method is the means of controlling the continuity from note to note. The material of music is sound and silence. Integrating these is composing."

Let's try it through again with substitutions where they may seem appropriate. Structure in poetry is its divisibility into successive parts, from phrases to longer sections. Form is content, the continuity or the morphology of continuity. Method is the means of controlling the continuity from word to word, or we might suggest from syllable to syllable, or more broadly from phrase to phrase, from line to line, et cetera. The material of poetry is sound and silence. That sounds good, I think. But, it's a difficulty. What sort of sound? The sound that words make only? The sound of syllables, the sound of nonsense? Other sounds also: sirens, perhaps? In any event, integrating whatever these may be is writing poetry. I wish I'd written a poem or two imitating the feasibility of the procedure, or the impossibility, or that I knew of examples of others which would illustrate the method. Although it may have been done already, if it has been, I am not acquainted with the results.

For all I know, though, poets all over the country at this very moment may be already tossing their coins. What I'm talking about, however, now, is a poetry that isn't yet written, so far as I know. Nevertheless we could try to describe, I believe, something of what it would be like when it was written. And we may find, if we look, examples from Cage's own writings which we will be very willing to call poetry, for whatever that no-longer-sacred title may mean. For one thing, such poetry may well have no recognizable beginnings, middles, and ends, being—again I'm using words from Cage taken somewhat out of context—being not preconceived objects but occasions for experience.

This introduces another aspect of Cage's theoretical contributions. In addition to exploiting the possibilities inherent in chance, it's also possible for similar motives to exploit those inherent in indeterminacy, especially in respect to the performance of the work. This or that aspect of the work may be controlled by chance. Some other aspect may be left indeterminate, with the result, for instance, that it may be new and unique at each performance. It's hard, again, to begin to think of poetry as, like music, something to be performed though it's, of course, easier today than it was 20 or 40 years ago, if not in ancient times or primitive cultures.

One possible way of resolving this difficulty is to think of the poet as he writes as, at that moment, in the act of performing his work. Another is, of course, to think of poetry as capable of moving toward theater, beginning to become involved with more than words as structured on a page, and requiring a kind of performance for its completion. In either event, the function of the performer, as Cage writes, is "comparable to that of someone filling in color where outlines are given." And he may perform his function in a way which is not consciously organized, either arbitrarily feeling his way, following the dictates of his ego, or more or less unknowingly, by going inwards, following, as in automatic writing, the dictates of his subconscious mind, or arbitrarily, by going outwards following his taste, or more or less unknowingly, by employing some operation exterior to his mind, some chance operation. This description seems to allow us the option of thinking of the poet as performer during the act of writing, since the acts described may be equally those of performer or composer in respect to music, "performer" within certain limits and toward certain ends such as those we've suggested.

Now in addition to unfamiliar formal structures, non-Aristotelian, such poetry might well embody what Cage calls the "coexistence of dissimilars." For instance, as possibilities very roughly analogous to the variables of musical sound, like frequency, amplitude, envelope, and so on. It might involve words at different levels of diction, or discontinuities of syntactical relations, or mixtures of kinds of material: narrative with lyrical, prosean loosely rhythmed with more highly rhythmed, and so on. And of course, we're not unfamiliar with such properties and usages in poetry already, especially in longer works by, say, Williams and Pound. But it's possible to distinguish purpose and method all the same, whether the end result much shows the distinction or not. And I'm not sure that it would or that it would matter if it did. When Williams inserts a large block of prose not notably relevant to its immediate surroundings, into Patterson, for instance, he's still following the dictates of his ego and going outwards, following his taste. He's not yet free of memory, psychology, or the traditions of the art of poetry. Later, we'll encounter a simpler example of such a "coexistence of dissimilars" in Olson. And examples of this feature do indeed abound in modern poetry, though seldom if ever so radical a degree as the Cage method would seem to be pointing toward.

Another feature of such poetry, though harder to pinpoint convenient parallels for it, would be implicit in Cage's remark that "in musical terms, any sound may occur in any combination and in any continuity." To substitute again, in poetic terms, any sound, any syllable, word, phrase, line, et cetera in any continuity is possible. Nonsense is suggested, or otherwise fragmented, disjointed discourse. Noise, the supposedly ugly, the cacophonous would be equally welcome along with the supposedly beautiful, the euphonious, and in any sequence. But if our basic ground for comparison, our basic point of reference is to remain the world of nature, and if the basic material for poetry is to be sound, sound and spaces between intended sounds that represent the pauses of relative silence, and sound is to be conceived of as words, an assumption which seems plausible if not obligatory, then what are these sounds or words in their natural state? For Williams, the answer was speech. But I'm by no means sure this would be the proper Cage answer. Words isolated from phrasal context as pure sound, nonsense or onomatopoetic exclamations as noise even grunts, snorts and the like—may these not likewise be included? Whether attractive or not scarcely matters at this stage of consideration. The dadaists tried out some of these possibilities years ago. Withers' poem of the repeated W comes to mind, since I just heard it for the first time the other night. And there may be other resources, other terms of conversion from one art to another waiting now to be found and used.

But if we think of the materials of poetry from a somewhat different angle, of words, say, in respect not to their sound exclusively but in whatever substantive referential character they may have, there's another and perhaps simpler solution to the problem. Not necessarily any more right than the other, but certainly simpler. What the words point to, the object of the world of nature, might be fitted into our formula in some such way as this. In terms of subject matter in poetry, any object in any combination and in any continuity. A surrealist passage or a passage from the writings of psychotics might be so described, I expect. Yet either would be only one kind of result and of a fairly fixed type, while the multiplicity of other types of result would remain available. The collages of painters offer several points of correspondence with the conceivable results. "Poetry," observes Cage, "is freewheeling." You get its impact by thumbing through any of the mass media. What I've been trying to describe as potential, however vaguely, is different, of course, from the mere practice of improvisation, in which poets, like composers or jazz musicians, have from time to time engaged, although I do know of a few examples of work done by young poets which, being improvised, allows for the inclusion of everything that happens during the act of composition, including so-called mistakes, even typos. But, this more resembles the old automatic writing or a dependence on the ego and the memory and the taste than what I have in mind. At any rate, while what we do have before us is a poetry of infinite possibilities, Cage's words describing Rauschenberg's painting, "where everything, even a pair of socks, is appropriate."

Now I want to turn from theory to some examples of poetry from Cage's writings. And I know the meaning of the word poetry keeps shifting as I'm using it today, perhaps disturbingly. But I don't feel that that, just now, is so bad a thing. Still, in looking for examples of poems by Cage, I have, I admit, consciously sought out passages which in one way or another would resemble our conventional ideas (mine, at least, which are conventional) as to what poetry is like. We know that some of his lectures themselves intend to say what he had to say in a way that would exemplify it, so that the listener might experience it rather than simply hear about it. And to do so, the lectures have employed methods also used in his musical compositions. The piece from which I take my first example, however, was written as a statement on dance, apparently to be read silently, that is, by the eye rather than performed as a lecture, that is, more theatrically, for the ear. It's perhaps for this reason he chose here to use the imperfections in the sheet of paper on which he worked as the basis for positioning in space the fragments to the text. It has, in other words, an appeal for the eye as, say, Mallarmé's "Un coup de des" does, or numerous later pieces of poetry. But since I am, so to speak, about to perform it orally, for the ear, and since in any case, I feel I am free, that is to say, indeterminate in respect to the performance, I'll chose only parts of the text to read, not the whole. The choice, unfortunately, perhaps depending on a going outwards, following my taste.

A bird flies
slavery is abolished
the woods.
a sound has no legs to stand on
the world is teeming anything can happen
the telephone rings
each person is in the best seat
War begins at any moment.
Is there a glass of water?
Each now is the time the space
lights in action
our eyes open
where the bird flies, fly
ears

Elsewhere, Cage observes in a lecture, "I have nothing to say and I am saying it and that is poetry." From the lecture "Indeterminacy," not as printed but as performed in the Folkways record, I have chosen three excerpts which I call poems, and I'll play them for you in a moment, as performed by the author, with David Tudor providing a background of other sounds: a small sample of poetry as theater. But remembering that Cage in distinguishing poetry from prose defined poetry as "more formalized," and particularly by reason of its allowing musical elements—sound, time—to be introduced into the world of words, I want to read you the examples first as prose, and especially because my tape is recorded at a very low level of sound and I'm not sure if you can hear the words as you should.

"[name] points out that a beautiful woman who gives pleasure to a man serves only to frighten the fish when she jumps in the water." That's number one. Number two: "Here's a large man falls asleep easily. One evening, driving back from Poughkeepsie, he awoke to say 'Now that everything's so easy there's so much to do.' Then he went back to sleep." Three: "Once I was visiting my Aunt Marge. She was doing her laundry. She turned to me and said, 'You know I love this machine much more than I do your Uncle Walter.'" Wait, you'll hear them as poetry in a minute. The entire lecture "Indeterminacy" is composed of stories, many types, of varying lengths, apparently. But, in performance, one story is told per minute. Time is introduced. Also, as regards structure, they're put together in an unplanned way to suggest, we're told, that all things are related and this complexity is more evident when it is not oversimplified by an idea of relationship in one person's mind. Thus I felt free again to choose my three examples not in sequence but in a discontinuity which, in small form, approximates the all-relatedness of things in nature and now in art as well.

[...]

I have one more example. The passage is taken from a piece of writing to appear in Cage's new book next fall, for which he, yesterday afternoon, very generously lent me proofs he had just received. And I say piece of writing because, for me, by now, as perhaps for you, genres are becoming rather pleasantly confused. Cage describes the piece this way: "a mosaic of ideas, statements, words and stories; also a diary. Chance operations were used to determine a variety of features of the text, including topography: twelve different typefaces." It's been given as a lecture but it is also, as the author tells me, something he considers poetry. So do I, though with this addendum: that it belongs in part—no reason it shouldn't—to that category for which a familiar literary critical term is didactic. As Cage himself has observed, with the sutras and shastras of India, information, no matter how stuffy, traditionally is transmitted by poetry, or can be. The title suggests as much. "Diary: How To Improve the World, You will Only Make Matters Worse, 1965." I choose, from taste and from ease of recognition, passages among the most obviously lyrical, though not without their mixtures, the coexistence of dissimilars.

> We see symmetrically
> Canoe a northern Canadian lake
> Mirrored our hearings
> As symmetrical
> Noticed sounds surprises

Echoes of shouts we make transform our
Voices straight line of sound from us to
shores followed by echoes slithering
around the lake's perimeter
when I
said
55 global services
California Bell telephone man replied
September 65 it's now 61
The seasons, creation
preservation, destruction, quiescence
This was experience in result an idea no
longer is he flies to Rio
What shall
we wear as we travel about
a summer suit?
With or without long underwear
What
about Stein's idea?
People are the way
Their land and air is

I better skip one passage I was going to read and go to later, from the 16th day.

Principles
Then all's intolerable
No principles.
Which doesn't mean we fail to become furious
So
We swim
Drowning now
and then
I must write and tell him
About beauty the urgency to avoid
it

And I imagine the similarities of such passages to what we familiarly call poetry must be evident, as well as some of the difference. What interests me now, for the purposes of this lecture, is neither its brilliance as writing nor, if you like, its possible lack of brilliance. That's beside the point, as the theory instructs us. It is. That it is the result, in part, of chance operations is interesting, though, in pointing toward what may happen when words are subjected to these. And one of the reasons for resorting to such a method, the blocking of the ego, has something in common with other motifs in contemporary poetry; that too is interesting. And that underlying this mixture of intention and non-intention is some idea that nature is like this; that art can be like nature: inclusive not exclusive. That anything can happen in it. For its pertinence, I really can't avoid one brief quotation from McLuhan, though, I'm sorry. "Today our science and method," he says, "strive not toward a point of view, a fixed or specialist point of view that would insist on repetition as the criterion of truth and practicality, but to discover how not to have a point of view. The method not of closure and perspective, but of the open field and suspended judgement." So too perhaps in poetry the field is open.

    [...]

    Olson is probably as close to the Cagean aesthetic in his poetry as any poet of reputation now writing. I'm not sure of that, but it seems, to me, probable. But, it occurs to me that we might, for this occasion, proceed one step further by subjecting a passage from Olson to a chance operation. And we might expect to find a more definitive exemplification of the kind of poetry indicated by Cage's theorizing about music. I know this is unfair to the Olson text, and I apologize. I did try the procedure first with some of my own writing, and it didn't seem to work at all. So, I have used this. I restricted myself to Letter 3 of the Maximus poems and, employing the coin toss method of chance operation, arrived at this brief example.

> Tansy for their noses
> From elsewhere that is my father did
> And not from the provinces
> With thee greyhounds aft the long diesels
> They play upon their bigotries
> Upon their fears
> Let them free the way for me
> For the men of the fort
> Tansy for their noses

I could've gone on but that seemed sufficient for the model or instance. And I did find this interesting in itself, and interesting is one result of method. Now, where do we go from here, Cage asks, as I do. His answer some years ago was: toward theater. That seems to me a very likely answer still. If it should lead to a blending or blurring of various kinds of art as we've known them, as I think we can see signs that it is doing, in the now-famous happenings, for instance, then we have the Cagean rationale for backing that art, theater, more than music, and we ought to add, more than poetry, et cetera, et cetera, resembles nature. Developments along such lines, I acknowledge, may lead to a dead end or various dead ends. In any plunge into the unknown, one may not know that one has arrived until he safely got back. And it's always easier to define an art already in existence than one coming into being, but redefinition may be in order for poetry now, a redefinition that will be more inclusive, more open. And at that, perhaps, the title of the lecture for today, taking one last cue from Cage, should've been, rather, "How to Improve Poetry: You Will Only Make Matters Worse, 1967." I don't know but I'll be interested in finding out.

Donald Justice
University of Cincinnati
February 1967

METRICAL TYPES IN ENGLISH

Traditional meters, having so distinctive a sound and being so well established by a consistent practice since the early Renaissance, would appear ready to yield at once to a descriptive analysis. This is, however, an illusion. Prosidists such as Sidney Lanier have understood the meters as measures of time; the majority, like George Saintsbury, have taken them to be measures of stress (i.e. accent). The nature of the language is so various, so many factors which go into its total sound are susceptible to some kinds of analysis—degrees—that a system of measure taking each of them into account, though perhaps practicable for the linguist, is unnecessarily complicated for the poet himself, even if in his own less scientific way he is obliged to consider them.

The poet is naturally under no obligation to become learned in prosody or even to memorize the standard classical names for metrical feet. Among some poets, indeed—even so learned a poet as Eliot, for example—it has been an affectation to protest one's innocence in such matters. In any event, the molossus and certain other classical feet have in the actual practice of English verse something of the mythical status of the griffin or the roc. For the poet who would write in traditional meters a good training of the ear on the practice of the masters (and his contemporaries) should be sufficient, no matter what set of terms he may choose to explain his practice and theirs. It is enough to be aware of what is possible so as to attempt that or something just beyond.

Nevertheless, we may try for the sake of clarification to describe modern practice with as simple and consistent a set of terms as we can. Although other prosodic bases have been tried in English, poets today write in meters that, for the sake of definition and convenience, we may call 1) Syllabic, 2) Accentual, 3) Accentual-Syllabic or 4) Free.

In **Syllabics** the norm of the line depends solely on a counting of the number of syllables. The number of stresses, not being a determining factor, will vary, and in theory it seems logical enough to suppose that it is to the advantage of Syllabics for the stress count to vary, so that the special and essential character of this metrical type may declare itself.

In **Accentuals** the norm of the line depends solely on a counting of the stresses (i.e. accents). The number of syllables is not a determining factor; their number will vary and—as with Syllabics—it may be supposed that it will be to the advantage of Accentuals for the syllable count to vary.

In **Accentual-Syllabics**—which seems a logical if somewhat awkward and artificial term for describing traditional meters—the norm of the line depends mutually on a counting of stresses and syllables both, and on a more or less regular alternation between the stressed and unstressed syllables.

In **Free Verse** any norm defined in terms of syllable-counting or stress-counting or some combination of both is non-existent. So long as none of the systems of measure, outlined above is to be employed, an incalculable number of "norms" may be devised; or none at all.

A SAMPLING OF SOME CLASSICAL
STATEMENTS REGARDING METER

...the origin of metre. This I would trace to the balance in the mind affected by that spontaneous effort which strives to hold in check the workings of passion. It might be easily explained likewise in what manner this salutary antagonism is assisted by the very state, which it counteracts; and how this balance of antagonists became organized into metre (in the usual acceptation of that term) by a supervening act of the will and judgment, consciously and for the foreseen purpose of pleasure.

...

...The EFFECTS of metre. As far as metre acts in and for itself, it tends to increase the vivacity and susceptibility both of the general feelings and of the attention. This effect it produces by the continued excitement of surprise, and by the quick reciprocations of curiosity still gratified and still re-excited, which are too slight indeed to be at any one moment objects of distinct consciousness, yet become considerable in their aggregate influence. As a medicated atmosphere, or as wine during animated conversation, they act powerfully, though themselves unnoticed.

...

But for any poetic purposes, metre resembles (if the aptness of the simile may excuse its meanness) yeast, worthless or disagreeable by itself, but giving vivacity and spirit to the liquor with which it is proportionately combined.

— Coleridge, from *Biographia Literaria*

Now the co-presence of something regular, something to which the mind has become accustomed in various moods and in a less excited state, cannot but have great efficacy in tempering and restraining the passion by an intertexture of ordinary feeling and of feeling not strictly and necessarily connected with the passion. This is unquestionable true; and hence, though the opinion will at first appear paradoxical, from the tendency of metre to divest language, in a certain degree, of its reality, and thus to throw a sort of half-consciousness of unsubstantial existence over the whole composition, there can be little doubt but that more pathetic situations and sentiments, that is, those which have a greater proportion of pain connected with them, may be endured in metrical composition, especially in rhyme than in prose.

. . .

...the various causes upon which the pleasure received from metrical languages depends. Among the chief of these causes is to be reckoned a principle which must be well known to those who have made any of the Arts the object of accurate reflection; namely, the pleasure which the mind derives from the perception of similitude in dissimilitude. This principle is the great spring of the activity of our minds and their chief feeder.

— Wordsworth (1800), from "Preface to Lyrical Ballads"

Rhythm and its specialized form, metre, depend upon repetition and expectancy.

. . .

Prose on the whole…is accompanied by a very much vaguer and more indeterminate expectancy than verse. In such prose as this page, for example, little more than a preparedness for further words not all exactly alike in sound and with abstract polysyllables preponderating is all that arises.

. . .

The sound gets its character by compromise with what is going on already.

. . .

This texture of expectations, satisfactions, disappointments, surprises, which the sequence of syllables brings about, is rhythm. And the sound of words comes to its full power only through rhythm. Evidently there can be no surprise and no disappointment unless there is expectation and most rhythms perhaps are made up as much of disappointments and postponements and surprises and betrayals as of simple, straightforward satisfactions. Hence the rapidity with which too simple rhythms, those which are too easily "seen through", grow cloying or insipid unless hypothetical states intervene, as with much primitive music and dancing and often with metre.

. . .

We may turn now to that more complex and more specialized form of temporal rhythmic sequence which is known as metre. This is the means by which words may be made to influence one another to the greatest possible extent. In metrical reading the narrowness and definiteness of expectancy, as much unconscious as ever in most cases, is very greatly increased, reaching in some cases, if rime is also used, almost exact precision.

. . .

…that a certain handling of metre should produce in a slight degree a hypnoidal state is not surprising. But it does so not as Coleridge suggests, through the surprise element in metrical effects, but through the absence of surprise, through the lulling

49

effects more than through the awakening. Many of the most characteristic symptoms of incipient hypnosis are present in a slight degree.

— I.A. Richards, from "Principles of Literary Criticism"

SYLLABICS

It has certain advantages, possible, for the purpose to which it is put in the Testament of Beauty over the heavily accented meter of Pound: its very monotony gives it a certain coherence, the coherence, however, merely of undefined intention, yet its freedom from the constant recurrence of the heavy measuring accent does not commit it so closely to a particular range of feeling.

—Yvor Winters, from In Defense of Reason

...a syllabic meter (is) determined by count of syllables only. It is, like the accentual, an old tradition in English; it accounts for the decasyllabic line of Wyatt and Donne:

> So, if I dream I have you, I have you.

and sometimes of Sidney:

> If you hear that they seem my heart to move

...

...observing only number (with some regard to accent)", as Sidney himself describes it. In the modern tradition it has these rules: the syllabification is that of ordinary educated speech, not of careful enunciation, and elision is optional. Final unaccented syllables count. And there is a negative principle, testifying to the power of traditional meter, that no succession of lines should establish the expectation of a repetitive stress pattern. Consequently, verses of seven or of nine syllables are best. It can handle the ordinariness of experience.

— J. V. Cunningham, from *Tradition and Poetic Structure*

METRICAL EXAMPLES

Je n'ais pas oublié, voisine de la ville,
Notre blanche maison, petite, mais tranquille;
Sa Pomone de platre et sa vielle Vénus
Dans un bosquet chétif cachant leurs members nus.

> — Baudelaire, from "Je n'ais pas oublié, voisine de la ville"
> (The Alexandrine: 12 syllables)

…She comes over the lawn, the young heiress,
From her early walk in the garden-wood,
Feeling that life's a table set to bless
Her delicate desires with all that's good,
That even the unopened future lies
Like a love-letter, full of sweet surprise.

> — Elizabeth Daryush, from "Still-life"

Dear son, when the warm multitudes cry,
But keep in mind the waters where fish
See scepters descending with no wish
To touch them; sit regal and erect,
But imagine the sands where a crown
Has the status of a broken-down
Sofa or mutilated statue:
Remember as bells and cannon boom
The cold deep that does not envy you,
The sunburnt superficial kingdom
Where a king is an object.

So, if you prosper, suspect those bright
Mornings when you whistle with a light
Heart. You are loved; you have never seen
The harbor so still, the park so green,
So many well-fed pigeons upon
Cupolas and triumphal arches,
So many stags and slender ladies
Beside the Canals. Remember when

Your climate seems a permanent home
For marvelous creatures and great men,
What griefs and convulsions startled Rome,
Ecbatans, Babylon.

—Auden, from "Alfonso to Ferdinand"

When eyeless fish meet her on
her way upward, they gently
turn together in the dark
brooks. But naked and searching
as a wind she will allow
no hindrance, none, and bursts up

through potholes and narrow flues
seeking an outlet. Unslowed
by fire, rock, water or clay,
she after a time reaches
the soft abundant soil...

—Thom Gunn, from "The Sea and The Land"

You have seen them, how
They stand there, perplexed,
...the lives they
Must have left somewhere
Once on a dresser—

— Charles Wright, from "The Daughters of Blum"

he said, When I have kicked off
and they cut me open, they
will find a dime-store diamond,

worthless, but reflecting light
where the heart is said to be.
And when we cut, we found it.

— Henri Coulette, from *The Collected Poems of Henri Coulette*

This has the ring of nonsense about it, no?
How can I tell you?
How can I explain to one
never there? I was a courier
and rode the Metro, disguised differently
every day. I was no one,

I was what I seemed, I did not have to think.
This house is the grave
Of Cinema, and this light
his epitaph. How can I explain
the dead? The dead are an extravagant cheese,
nor have the sad gift of tongues.

— Henri Coulette, from *The Collected Poems of Henri Coulette*

Berry rotten
In ripeness
Where we
Lay,
What
After
Late motions
Of the sun, what
Grief on the hills…

— Richard Howard

The cancellings, the negations are never
ultimate, are never one last wipe
that clears the lens, a farewell
to supersession, finale of ruin.

Is it because spirit is not strong enough
to forgive flesh? The pardon that comes
must come (if it comes) because
flesh forgives spirit. That is the work of prose…

— Richard Howard, from "Prose for Borges"

...No swan
with swart blind look askance
and gondoliering lets, so fine
   as the chintz china one with fawn-
brown eyes and toothed gold
collar on to show whose bird it was.

        — Marianne Moore, from "No Swan So Fine"

Now as I was young and easy under the apple boughs
About the lilting house and happy as the grass was green,
   The night about the dingle starry,
    Time let me hail and climb
   Golden the heydays of his eyes,
And honored among wagons I was prince of the apple towns

       Trail with daisies and barley
       Down the rivers of the windfall light.

And as I was green and carefree, famous among the barns
About the happy yard and singing as the farm was home,
    In the sun that is young once only
   Time let me lay and be
Golden in the mercy of his means,
And green and golden I was huntsman and herdsman, the calves
Sang to my horn, the foxes on the hills barked clear and cold,
And the Sabbath rang slowly
In the pebbles of his holy streams...

        — Dylan Thomas, from "Fern Hill"

Overnight, very
Whitely, discreetly,
Very quietly

Our toes, our noses
Take hold on the loam,
Acquire the air.

Nobody sees us,
Stops us, betrays us;
The small grains make room.

— Sylvia Plath, from "Mushrooms"

...we go
ahead and
kiss. She is
fine glass, I
say, throwing
her to the
floor...

— James Tate, from "The Mirror"

Su luna de pergamino
Preciosa tocando viene
por un anfibio sender
de cristales y laurels.
El silencio sin estrellas,
huyendo del sononete,
cae donde el mar bate y canta
su noche llena de peces.
En los picos de la sierra
los carabineros duermen
guardando las blancas torres
donde viven los ingleses...

Deeply influenced by the folk poetry of Spain, Lorca wrote these
poems in one of the oldest of popular rhythms, the eight-syllable
ballad line—not to be thought of as corresponding to the
English lines of four iambic or trochaic feet, since in the Spanish
line there is no pattern of accents: only the seventh syllable is
accented regularly. The stanzas do not rhyme, but all the even-
numbered lines are linked by assonance. Throughout 'Preciosa
and the Air,' for example, the two final vowel sounds are *e-e*, as

in *viene, laureles.* The Spanish reader hears in Lorca's ballads the energetic rhythms long familiar, but he is aware at the same time of something new and strange.

— J.F. Nims, from *The Poem Itself*

AHAB: Lad, lad, I tell thee
thou must not follow
Ahab now. The hour
is coming when Ahab would
yet would not have thee
by him. There is that
in thee, poor lad, which
I feel too curing
to my malady...

PIP: No, no, no! ye have
not a whole body,
sir; do ye but use
poor me for your one
lost leg; only tread
upon me, sir; I
ask no more, so I
remain part of ye.

— Melville, from *Moby Dick*

ACCENTUALS (OR STRESS VERSE)

Old English poetry consists of lines divided into verses by a pause or caesura, the two verses being bound together by alliteration...

The most essential element of Old English meter is the natural stress of the spoken language, the rules of sentence-stress as well as word-stress being rigorously observed...

Each normal verse has two strong-stressed elements or lifts...

It will be understood that all the lifts in a line need not—and indeed cannot—be all equal stress...

Stress and alliteration are inseparably connected in Old English meter: in every verse the two words which have strongest natural stress must join in the alliteration...

The great variety which we observe in the structure of Old English verse is the result not only of its laxity as regards the number of syllables, but also of the freedom with which the elements of the verse—the lifts and dips (i.e. the weakly stressed elements, contrasting with the lifts, or strongly stressed elements)—are combined.

> ...the meter of Christabel is not, properly speaking, irregular, though it may seem so from its being founded on a new principle: namely, that of counting in each line the accents, not the syllables. Though the latter may vary from seven to twelve, yet in each line the accents will be found to be only four. Nevertheless, this occasional variation in number of syllables is not introduced wantonly, or for the mere ends of convenience, but in correspondence with some transition in the nature of the imagery or passion.
>
> — Coleridge, from his preface to *Christabel*

Sprung Rhythm, as used in this book, is measured by feet of from one to four syllables, regularly, and for particular effects any number of weak or slack syllables may be used. It (each foot) has one stress, which falls on the only syllable, if there is only one, or, if there are more, then…on the first, and so gives rise to four sorts of feet, a monosyllable and the s-called accentual Trochee, Dactyl and the First Paeon….nominally the feet are mixed and any one may follow any other….any two stresses may either follow one another running or be divided by one, two or three slack syllables…In Sprung Rhythm…the feet are assumed to be equally long or strong and their seeming inequality is made up by pause or stressing…

Sprung Rhythm is the most natural of things. For (1) it is the rhythm of common speech and of written prose, when rhythm is perceived in them. (2) It is the rhythm of all but the most monotonously regular music, so that in the words of choruses and refrains and in songs written closely to the music it arises. (3) It is found in nursery rhymes, weather saws, and so on; because, however these may have been once made…, the terminations having dropped off by the change of language, the stresses come together and so the rhythm is sprung. (4) It arises in common verse when reversed or counterpointed…

– G. M. Hopkins, from his own preface to his manuscript

Theoretically the problem is this, whether in poetry the speech as determined by its accent rhythm can e made so persistently beautiful in form as to dispense with all the subtle assistance which it derives from interplay with a fundamental metrical form…A question arises…whether, if the speech-rhythm be the beauty of the verse, it may not be a sufficient rule for it; whether indeed, the rhythm of *Paradise Lost*, and *Samson*…are any the better for their strict syllabic scheme and prosodial fiction.

– Robert Bridges, from *Milton's Prosody*

METRICAL EXAMPLES

Es treibt mkich hin, es treibt mich her?
Noch wenige Stunden, den sol lich sie schauen,
Sie selber, die schonste der schonen Jungfrauen; –
Du treues Herz, was pochst du so schwer!

Hwaet, we Gar-Dena   in gear-dagum
Theod-cyninga   thrym gefrunon,
Hu tha athelingas   Ellen fremedon.
Oft Scyld Scefing   sceathena threatum,
Monegum maegthem   meodo-setla ofteah.
Egsode eorl,   syththan aerest wearth
Feasceaft funden   he thas frofre gebad
Weox under wolcnun,   weorth-myndum thah,
Oth that him aeghwylc   thara ymb-sittendra
Ofer hron-rade   hyran scolde,
Gomban gyldan——   that was god cyning!

List to an old-time lay of the Spear-Danes,
Full of the prowess of famous kings,
Deeds of renown that were done by the heroes.
From raiders a-many their mead-halls wrested.
He lived to be feared, though first as a waif,
Puny and frail he was found on the shore.
He grew to be great, and was girt with power
Till the order-tribes all obeyed his rule,
And sea-folk hardy that sit by the whale-road
Gave him tribute, a good king he was.

– from Beowulf

In a somer seson, whan soft was the sonne,
I shope me into shroudes, as I a shepe were;
In habite as an heremite unholy of works
Ac on a May morning on malverne hulles
Me bifel a ferly, of fairy me thoughte:
I was very forwandred and went me to reste

Under a brode banke by a bornes side,
And as I lay and lened and loked on the wateres,
I slombred in a sleping, it swayed so merye.

—William Langland, from Piers Plowman

Adam lay yboundin, boundin in a bond,
Foure thousand winter thought he not to long.
And al was for an appil, an appil that he took,
As clerkes findin wretin in here book.

—Anonymous

Peas porridge hot, peas porridge cold,
Peas porridge in the pot, nine days old.

—Anonymous

Somtime he would gaspe
Whan he saw a waspe;
A fly or a gnat,
He wolde flye at that;
An pritely he wold pant
When he saw an ant;
Lord, how he wold pry
After the butterfly!
Lorde, how he wolde hop
After the gesso!

— John Skelton, from "The Book of Philip Sparrow"

'O where hae ya been, my dearest dear,
    These seven lang years and more?
'O I am come to seek my former vows
    Ye granted me before.

She had sailed a league, a league,
    A league but barely twa,
Till she did mind on the husband she left
    And her wee young son alsua.

He's tane her by the milk-white hand
    And he's thrown her in the main;
And full five and twenty hundred ships
    Perished all on the coast of Spain.

                         — Anonymous

It is an ancient Mariner,
And he stoppeth one of three.
'By thy long grey beard and glittering eye,
Now wherefore stopp'st thou me?'

The ship was cheered, the harbor cleared,
Merrily did we drop
Below the kirk, below the hill,
Below the lighthouse top.

Higher and higher every day,
Till over the mast at noon—
The Wedding-Guest here beat his breast,
For he heard the loud bassoon.

        — Coleridge, from *The Rime of the Ancient Mariner*

'Tis the middle of the night by the castle clock,
And the owls have awakened the crowing cock
Tu-whit!—Tu-whoo!
And hark, again! the crowing cock;
How drowsily it crew.

Sir Leoline, the Baron rich,
Hath a toothless mastiff bitch;
From her kennel beat the rock
She maketh answer to the clock,
Four for the quarters, and twelve for the hour;

Ever and aye, by shine and shower,
Sixteen short howls, not ever loud;
Some say, she sees my lady's shroud.

Is the night chilly and dark?
The night is chilly, but not dark.

— Coleridge, from *Christabel*

I am sick, I must die.

—Thomas Nash, from "In Time of Pestilence, 1593"

Up I start, forth when I,
With her face to feed mine eye.

— Robert Greene, "The Palmer's Ode"

Jesus, heart's light,
       Jesus, maid's son,
What was the feast followed the night
       Thou hadst glory of this nun?
Feast of the one woman without stain.
For so conceived, so to conceive thee is done;
       But here was heart-throe, birth of a brain,
  Word, that heard and kept thee and uttered thee outright.

       Well, she has thee for the pain, for the
       Patience; but pity of the reset of them!
Heart, go and bleed at a bitterer vein for the
       Comfortless, unconfessed of them—
No not uncomforted: lovely-felicitious Providence
Finger of a tender of, O of a feathery delicacy, the breast of the
       Maiden could obey so, be a bell to, ring of it, and
Startle the poor sheep back! Is the shipwreck then a harvest, does tempest
       Carry the grain for thee?

. . .

Earnest, earthless, equal, atoneable, vault, voluminous, . . . stupendous
  With: Our evening is over us; our night whelms, and will end us.
  Where, selfrung, selfstrung, sheathe- and shelterless, thoughts against thoughts
                    in groans grind.

          – Hopkins from "The Wreck of the Deutschland"

Margaret, are you grieving?
Over Goldengrove unleaving?
Leaves, like the things of man, you
With your fresh thoughts care for, can you?
Ah! as the heart grows older
It will come to such sights colder
By and by, nor spare a sigh
Thought worlds of wanwood leafmeal lie;
And yet you will weep and know why.
Now, no matter, child, the name:
Sorrow's springs are the same.
Nor mouth had, no nor mind, expressed
What heart heard of, ghost guessed:
It is the blight man was born for,
It is Margaret you mourn for.

          – Hopkins, from "Spring and Fall"

High were those headlands; the eagles promised
Life without lawyers. Our long convoy
Turned away northward as tireless gulls
Wove over water webs of brightness
And sad sound. The insensible ocean,
Miles without mind, moaned all around our
Limited laughter . . .

          – Auden, from "The Age of Anxiety"

Bending forward
With stern faces
Pilgrims puff
Up the steep bank
In huge hats.

Shouting, I run
In the other direction,
Cheerful, unchaste,
With open shirt
And tinkling guitar.

— Auden, from "The Age of Anxiety"

Is it less than our brilliance, Ishtar,
How the snowfield smarts in the fresh sun,
And the bells of its melting ring, and we blink
    At the light flexing in trickles?

It is the Spring's disgrace
That already, before the prone arbutus
Will risk its whiteness, you have come down
    To the first gate and darkened.

Forgive us, who cannot conceive you
Elsewhere and maiden, but love you only
Fallen among us in rut and furrow,
    In the shade of amassing leaves,

— Richard Wilbur, from "To Ishtar"

Many poets writing accentual verse do not attempt to avoid the
iambic pattern which recurs so easily; often the result is a rather
hybrid sort of verse, hovering between the standard metrical
system and a purely accentual rule.

— J. McAuley

I have met them at close of day
Coming with vivid faces
From counter or desk among grey
Eighteenth-century houses.
I have passed with a nod of the head
Or polite meaningless words,
Or have lingered awhile and said
Polite meaningless words,

And thought before I had done
Of a mocking tale or a gibe
To please a companion
Around the fire at the club,
Being certain that they and I
But lived where motley is worn:
All changed, changed utterly:
A terrible beauty is born.

—Yeats, from "Easter, 1916"

I sit in one of the dives
On Fifty-Second Street
Uncertain and afraid
As the clever hopes expire
Of a low dishonest decade:
Waves of anger and fear
Circulate over the bright
And darkened lands of the earth,
Obsessing our private lives;
The unmentionable odor of death
Offends the September night.

— Auden, from "September 1, 1939"

Where were you last night? I watched at the gate;
I went down early, I stayed down late.
Were you snug at home, I should like to know,
Or were you in the coppice wheedling Kate?

— Christina Rossetti, from "Last Night"

Dipodic Verse: Verse constructed rhythmically so that, in scansion, pairs of feet must be considered together. That is, the metrical unit is less the individual foot than a dipody (2 related but slightly dissimilar feet, one of which normally has a stronger stress than the other). Crude dipodic verse, of the sort encountered in children's rhymes, nursery songs, and popular ballads, provide simple examples.

— *Princeton Encyclopedia of Poetry and Poetics*

Peas porridge hot, peas porridge cold,
Peas porridge in the pot, nine days old.

Taffy was a Welshman, Taffy was a thief.

Dirty British coaster with a salt-caked smoke stack,
Butting through the Channel in the mad March days,
With a cargo of Tyne coal,
Road-rails, pig-lead,
Firewood, iron-ware, and cheap tin trays.

— John Masefield, from "Cargoes"

I must go down to the seas again, to the lonely sea and the sky,
And all I ask is a tall ship and a star to steer her by,
And the wheel's kick and the wind's song and the white sail's shaking,
And a gray mist on the sea's face and a gray dawn breaking.

— John Masefield, from "Sea Fever"

Dim drums throbbing, in the hills half heard,
Where only on a nameless throne a crownless prince has stirred,
Where, risen from a doubtful seat and half attained stall,
The last knight of Europe takes weapons from the wall,
The last and lingering troubadour to whom the bird has sung...
Strong gongs groaning as the guns boom far,
Don John of Austria is going to the war,
Stiff flags straining in the night-blasts cold,
In the gloom-black purple, in the glint old-gold,
Torchlight crimson the copper kettle-drums,
Then the tickets, then the trumpets, then the cannon, and he comes...

— G.K. Chesterton, from "Lepanto"

But I must now summarize my position in general terms. The sum total of metrical virtues is ... a profound advantage ... to the ... lyric. The sum total may be described briefly as follows: coherence of movement, variety of movement, and find perceptivity. These virtues can occur in conjunction only if a system is based (as English verse is normally based) on accent, then every syllable must be recognizably in or out of place whether stressed or not, and if out of place in a classifiable way; the degree of accent must vary perceptibly though immeasurable from a perceptible though immeasurable norm; quantity should be used consciously to qualify these conditions; in brief, the full sound-value of every syllable must be willed for a particular end, and must be precise in the attainment of that end. As language has other values than those of sound, this ideal will be always forced into some measure of compromise with the other values; nevertheless, the essence of art, I take it, is that no compromise should be very marked, and the perfection of art, though rare and difficult, is not unattainable. In a system such as English syllabics, or as free verse, most or all of the individual syllables can have no definite relationship to the pattern; so that there is no exact basis for judging them, and they are, when chosen, relatively without meaning.

Traditional meter, then, like the other aspects of traditional convention...tends to exploit the full possibilities of language... as traditional poetry in general aims to adjust feeling rightly to motive, it needs the most precise instrument possible for the rendering of feeling, and so far as meter is concerned, this instrument will be traditional meter. Further, as traditional poetry tends to enrich itself with past wisdom, with an acquired sense of what is just, so the traditional meters, owing to their very subtle adjustability and suggestibility, are frequently very complex in their effect...

Such a poem is a perfect and complete act of the spirit; it calls upon the full life of the spirit; it is difficult of attainment, but I am aware of no good reason to be contented with less.

—Yvor Winters, from In Defense of Reason

Once the metrical pattern is clear, it goes on in our mind as a pattern of expectation, able to resolve ambiguous syllables in its favor, and able at times to overcome the slight reluctance of an occasional phrase to take the required shape—so long as the reluctance is not too great.

What we must insist on, therefore, is that the scansion is not an attempt to give a full account of the rhythmic behavior of the syllables of spoken verse, and in particular it is not meant to be an adequate notation of stress-values. It has the much simpler task of referring the line to the metrical code under which it operates, giving each syllable the value it acquires within that code (always allowing for variations permitted by the code).

But what is the role of metre if it is this semi-abstract sort of thing, not a comprehensive formula for the actual movement of spoken verse? Its role is to provide a fixed scheme, across which the endless variety of stress-fluctuations can play as one therefore not a single and simple thing but essentially dual; comprising a simultaneous recognition on the one hand of the constant metrical pattern (with its occasional variations by substitution of feet), and on the other of the actual stress-profile of the line as natural speech would require. These two experiences are mated, they are coherent; they are not *radically* distinct since metre is rooted in stress. But they are not identical, and a true feeling for verse depends on appreciating the difference.

Contrast, but not contradiction; freedom within order; variety within uniformity; tension and flexibility; the unexpected that nevertheless fulfills the pattern it seems to be overriding; the heightened notice ability of each syllable because its actual behavior is upon a basis of regular expectation; the reconciling of the natural and the artificial in the dance of language; the sensitive response to logical and emotional nuance—these are the reasons that have made accentual-syllabic verse one of the great Inventions of Western culture, and have enabled its usefulness to endure over many centuries.

When we say that our experience of the line of verse is dual, we are implying (a) that the verse is not spoken simply in accordance with the *tom-tom tom-tom* of the metical scheme, but also, (b) that it is not spoken simply in accordance with the distribution of stress that it would have in conversation or if read as a piece of prose. The actual spoken line is really a third thing, the reconciliation of the related but competing demands ... verse is neither a mechanical sing-song of words dominated by the metre, nor is it ordinary speech unmodified by the presence of metrical pattern. We have seen how the natural stress-pulsations reveal to us the underlying metre; but in turn the metre once established exerts an influence upon our rendering of stress: the actual line is a resultant, a compromise, a thing *sui generis*; it is speech that has entered into the condition of formal art, the dance of words.

— James McAuley, from *Versification*

Metre is the sign that the language of the poem is an imitation. When the elements of language chosen to make the metre and the elements of language inherent in the speech the poet must use are brought together in the poem, they exist there in such a way that they imply one another, and yet retain their separate identities. It is thus that the language of speech is made into art, if art is imitation. For what poetry imitates is the structure of the language itself, this great system of sounds we use so cleverly, transmitting our signals to one another about everything in the universe.

— John Thompson, from *The Founding of English Metre*

The descriptive problems raised can be avoided by regarding a meter, not as a schematic diagram of scansions, but as a collection of syllabic-syntactic types; any one fulfills the law. Any line of the type, "A rosy garland and a weary head," is an iambic pentameter; for example, "The raving beauty or the common scold." And, indeed, it is the way we perceive meter when we read without hesitation or analysis, that is, poetically. We do not hear diagrams.

Again, traditional meter is felt to be artificial, which, of course, is why it is used, and to exclude the natural rhythms of real speech. It is said again and again, as if it were true, that people do not talk in iambic pentameters. But they do; not always, but often enough. Some months ago I sat in the sun and wrote down these lines at random. They are segments of real speech:

I'll have the special and a glass of milk
The order will be ready when you come.
We ought to be in Cleveland in an hour.
I haven't anything to say to you.
Goddamn it, what the hell is going on?
I'll think it over and I'll let you know.
Oh, go to hell! Who do you think you are?
She does her exercises every day.
How often shall I see you in a lifetime?

But perhaps most people talk in the octosyllabic line, in iambic tetrameters:

I love her and I always will.
Young poets are a dime a dozen.
I'll be there anytime you say.
He doesn't love me anymore.
For Christ's sake, will you stop that noise?
I didn't ask you what you thought.
I've had a headache for two days.
Darling, I'd rather not tonight.
What's playing at the Paramount?
I put five dollars on the nose.
Some people do, some people don't.

Is there a doctor in the house?
We live in Massachusetts now.
Who do you think you are? The Pope?

If the ear for iambic pentameter and tetrameter has not been completely destroyed in our society, you will have heard each of these lines as simultaneously a completed grammatical segment and one of the various types of recognizable iambic lines. It is encoded not only in grammar, but also at the same time in meter, for meter is the principle or set of principles, whatever they may be, that determines the line. Consequently, grammar and prosody are separate concurrent principles of the same order. And as we perceive of each sentence, without stopping to analyze it, that it is grammatical or not, so the repetitive perception that this line is metrical or that it is not, that it exemplifies the rules of its meter or that it does not, is the metrical experience.

— J. V. Cunningham, from *The Collected Essays of J. V. Cunningham*

THE SO-CALLED "PERMISSIVE VARIATIONS"

Based on a reading of more than four centuries of verse in English (from, say, 1557 to the present), and considering chiefly verse composed in iambic feet (the principal foot during this time), we may observe that the following variations on the iambic base or norm constitute *in practice* virtually every departure from that base. (This attempt at a sort of codification does not proceed from a desire to regulate or impose a theory but from an attempt to describe in the simplest possible terms what poets from the time of Surrey and Sidney to the time of Stevens or, later, Wilbur and Hecht have in fact put into practice.) Iambic pentameter –or five-foot line—has been the most common line in practice and therefore forms the basis for the following descriptive list.

1. The iamb is simply reversed, especially in the first foot of the line. The iamb is sometimes reversed in other positions in the line, often after a pause and usually even then in the middle of the line (that is, in the third or fourth foot). Reversals of the second foot are infrequent, of the fifth foot very rare. Two such reversals in successive feet are rare, as are reversals of more than two feet anywhere in a given line.

2. Two weakly stressed syllables replace the single weakly stressed syllable of the iamb (or the reversed iamb), and especially (some would say exclusively) does this occur where elision of one of the weakly stressed syllables is possible. There is precedent for many of the "poetical" elisions in our speech habits when dealing with certain combinations of sounds. Examples of poetical elision (that is, of words whose syllable count may be reduced, at least theoretically but also on occasion in practice, by a gliding together of certain syllable): *being, riot* (y-glide), *ruinous, followers, shadowy* (w-glide), *murmuring, reason* (semi-vowels). Also by convention such verbal sequences as *of the, in the,* and the like, which in the past were shown in print as *o'the, i'the.* This now superfluous apostrophe to show elision other cases (*e'er* for *ever,* e.g.) appears in Renaissance texts and many others through the Romantic period at least.

3. An extra (non-metrical) weakly stressed syllable—sometimes two or more—is commonly added at the end of a line, the so-called feminine ending; or, occasionally, after a definite pause in the middle of a line. (This latter type of extra syllable turns out to be identical in practice to #21, above, in effect).

4. What John Crowe Ransom and others have called an "ionic" or double foot replaces two successive iambs ˘ ˘ ′ ′ ; ′ ′ ˘ ˘.

5. *Rare.* The first weakly stressed syllable is dropped or, even more rarely, a weakly stressed syllable elsewhere, especially in Chaucer or recent verse. The result is usually called a headless line.

Some common types of feet or sequences of feet, which may be described in a variety of ways but which are, in any case, normal metrical occurrences:

1. The Ambiguous Foot. For ˘ ´ some will read ´ ˘; or ˘ ˘.
2. The Possible Spondee. For ˘ ´; or ´ ˘ some will read ´ ´.
3. The So-called Ionic. For ˘ ´ ˘ ´ or ´ ˘ ˘ ´ some will read ˘ ˘ ´ ´; ´ ´ ˘ ˘.

METRICAL EXAMPLES

Note: some early examples may be viewed more as historical precedents than as finished examples of the meters.

> And as it were halving a-game.
> Sche axeth me what is my name.
> "Ma dame," quod sche, "in my power"
> Thou most as of thy love stoned;
> For I thy bille have understonde
> In which to Cupide and to me
> Somdiel thou hast compleigned thee,
> But somdiel to Nature also.
> But that schal stoned among you tow,
> For thereof have I noght to done;
> For Nature is under the mone
> Maitresse of every lives kinde.

> — John Gower, from "Confessio Amantis"

> And whan he rood, men myghte his brydel here
> Ginglen in a whistling wynde als cleere
> And eek as loude as dooth the chapel belle.
> There as this lord was keeper of the celle,
> The rule of saint Maure or of saint Benefit,
> By cause that it was old and somdel street
> This ilke Monk leet olde things pace,
> And heeld after the newe world the space.

> — Chaucer (1343 – 1400) from "A Monk"

> And for ther is so gret diversity
> In Englissh and in writing of oure tonge,
> So prey I God that non miswrite the,
> Ne the mysmetre for defaute of tonge.
> And red whereto thaw be, or ells singe,
> That thaw be understonde, God I bineche!
> But yet to purpose of my rather speech.—

> — Geoffrey Chaucer, from "Troilus and Criseyde"

a) It was no derma: I lay brode waking.   ms.
b) It was no derma: for I lay broader awaking.   Total

a)The powar of them, to whom fortune hath lent.   ms.
b)The power of them: whom fortune here hath lent. Total

a) That railed rekles to every mans shame.   ms.
b) That railed rechlesse unto ech mans shame.   Total

            —Wyatt (1503 – 1542), from *Total's Miscellany*

Who so list to haunt, I knower were is an hynde,
    But as for me, helas, I may no more:
The vane travail hath wearied me so sore.
    I am of theism that farthest commeth behind;
Yet may I by no meanes my wearied mined
    Drawe from the Deere: but as she fleet afore,
    Fainting I folowe. I leve of therefore,
    Sins in a nett I seke to hold the wined.
Who list her hount, I put him owe of dowbte,
    As well as I may spend his tyme in vaine:
    And graven with Diamonds, in letters plain
There is written her faier neck rounde abowte:
    Nolin me tangere, for Cesars I ame;
    And wiled for to hold, though I seme tame.

   —Wyatt, from "Whose List to Hunt, I Know Where is an Hind"

Lyke as a huntsman after weary chance
Seeing the game from his escape away,
Sits down to rest him some shady place,
With panting hounds beguiled of their pray:
So after long pursuit and vainer assay,
When I all weary had the chance forooke,
The gentle deare returnd the self-same way,
Thinking to quench her thirst at the next brooke.
There she beholding me with milder looke,
Sought not to fly, but fearless still did bide:
Till I in hand her yet halfe trembling tooke,

And with her owne goodwill hir fyrmely tyde.
Strange thing me seemd to see a beast so wild,
So goodly wonne with her owne will beguiled.

— Spenser, from "Amoretti"

With how sad steps, o Moone, thou climb's the skies,
How silently, and with how wane a face,
What may it be, tha even in heav'ly place
That busier archer his sharpe arrows tries?
Sure if that long with *Love* acquainted eyes
Can judge of *Love*, thou feels a Lover's case;
I read it in thy looks, thy languish grace
To me that feele the like, thy state descries.

— Sidney (1554—1586), from *Strophe and Stella*

You Gote-herd Gods, that love the grassie mountains,
You Nymphs that haunt the springs in pleasant valise,
You Satyrs yoyde with free and quiet forests,
Vouchsafe your silent eares to playing musique,
Which to my woes gives still an early morning:
And drawes the dolor on till wery evening.

These mountains witness shall, so shall these vallies,
These forests eke, made wretched by our musique,
Our morning hymne is this, and song at evening.

— Sidney, from *The Countess of Pembroke Arcadia*

It was then night: the sound and quiet sleep
Had through the earth the wearied bodies caught;
The woods, the raging seas were fallen to rest;
When that the stars had half their course declined
The fields whist; beasts and fowls of divers hue,
And what so that in the broad lakes remained,

Or yet among the busy thicks of briar
Laid down to sleep by silence of the night,
Can 'suage their cares, mindless of travels past.

> — Surrey, from *The Aeneid*
> (his translation was the first blank verse in English)

Why, this is hell, nor am I out of it.
Think'st thou that I who saw the face of God
And tasted the eternal joys of heaven,
Am not tormented with ten thousand hells
In being deprived of everlasting bliss?
O Faustus, leave these frivolous demands,
Which strikes a terror to my fainting soul.

> — Marlow, from *Doctor Faustus*

That time of year thou mayst in me behold
When yellow leaves, or none, or few, do hang
Upon those boughs that shake against the cold,
Bare ruined choirs where late the sweet birds sang ...

> — Shakespeare, from "Sonnet 73"

When to the sessions of sweet silent thought
I summon up remembrance of things past,
I sign the lack of many a thing I sought,
And with old woes new wail my dear time's waste ...

> — Shakespeare, from "Sonnet 30"

Heaven is here
Where Juliet lives; and every cat and dog
And little mouse, every unworthy thing,
Live here in heaven and may look on her;
But Romeo may not. More validity,
More honorable state, more courtship lives
In carrion flies than Romeo. They may seize
On this white wonder of dear Juliet's hand

And steal immortal blessing from her lips,
Who, even in pure and vestal modesty,
Still blush, as thinking their own kisses sin:
But Romeo may not—he is banished …
O friar, the damned use that word in hell:
Howling attends it! How hast thou the heart,
Being a divine, a ghostly confessor,
A sin-absolver, and my friend profess'd,
To mangle me with that word banished?

— Shakespeare, from *Romeo and Juliet*

O Proserpina,
For the flowers now, that frighted thou let'st fall
From Dis's wagon! Daffodils,
That come before the swallow dares and take
The winds of March with beauty: violets—dim,
But sweeter than the lids of Juno's eyes
Or Cytherea's breath; pale primroses,
That die unmarried ere they can behold
Bright Phoebus I his strength (a malady
Most incident to maids); bold oxlips and
The crown imperial; lilies of all kinds,
The flower-de-luce being one! O, these I lack.

— Shakespeare, from *The Winter's Tale*

And so we may arrive to Talmud skill
And profane Greek to raise the building up
Of Helen's house against the Ismaelite,
King of Thogarma, and his habergeons
Brimstony, blue and fiery; and the force
Of King Abandon, and the beast of Cittim;
Which Rabbi David Kimchi, Onkelos,
And Aben Ezra do interpret Rome.

— Ben Jonson, from *The Alchemist*

Not content with such
Audacious neighborhood, the wisest heart

Of Solomon he led by fraud to build
His temple right against the Temple of God
On that opprobrious hill; and made his grove
The pleasant valley of Hinnom, Tophet, thence,
And black Gehenna called, the type of Hell.
Next Chemo's, the obscene dread of Moab's sons,
From Aroer to Nebo, and the wild
Of southmost Horonaim, Seon's realm, beyond
The flowery dale of Sigma clad with vines,
And Eleale, to the Asphaltic Pool.

                — Milton, from *Paradise Lost*

Yet once more, O ye laurels, and once more,
Ye myrtles brown, with ivy never sere,
I come to pluck your berries harsh and crude,
And with forced fingers rude
Shatter your leaves before the mellowing year.

Bring the rathe primrose that forsaken dies,
The tufted crow-toe, and pale Jessamine,
The white pink, and the pansy freaked with jet,
The glowing violet,
The must-rose, and the well atired woodbine.

Look homeward angel now, and melt with ruth:
And, O ye dolphins, waft the hapless youth.
Weep no more, woeful shepherds, weep no more,
For Lycidas your sorrow is not dead,
Sunk though he be beneath the watery floor.

                — Milton, from "Lycidas"

Ashamed to own they gave delight before,
Reduced to feign it, when they give no more:
As Hags hold Sabbath, less for joy than spite,
So these their merry, miserable night;
Still round and round the Ghosts of Beauty glide,
And haunt the places where their Honor died.

                — Pope, from "Epistle to a Lady"

Shut, shut the door, good John! Fatigued, I said,
Tie up the knocker, say I'm sick, I'm dead,
The Dog-Star rages! Nay, 'tis past a doubt,
All Bedlam, or Parnassus, is let out:
Fire in each eye, and papers in each hand,
They rave, recite, and madden round the land.
What walls can guard me, or what shades can hide?
They pierce my thickets, though my Grot they glide;
By land, by water, they renew the charge;
They stop the chariot, and they board the barge.

— Pope, from "An Epistle to Arbuthnot"

Sometimes it befell
In these nigh wanderings, that a strong desire
O'erpowered my better reason, and the bird
Which was the captive of another's toll
Became my prey; and when the deed was done
I heard among the solitary hills
Low breathings coming after me, and sounds
Of undistinguishable motion, steps
Almost as silent as the turf they trod.

— Wordsworth, from *The Prelude*

Magnificient
The morning was, a memorable pomp,
More glorious than I ever had beheld.
The sea was laughing at a distance; all
The solid mountains were as bright as clouds.

Magnificient
The morning rose, in memorable pomp,
Glorious as e'er I had beheld—in front,
The sea lay laughing at a distance; near,
The solids mountains shone, bright as the clouds.

— Wordsworth, from "Resolution and Independence"

Earth has not anything to show more fair:
Dull would he be of soul who could pass by
A sight so touching it its majesty;
This city now doth, like a garment, wear
The beauty of the morning: silent, bare,
Ships, towers, domes, theatres, and temples lie
Upon unto the fields, and to the sky;
All bright and glittering in the smokeless air.
Never did sun so beautifully steep
In his first splendor, valley, rock, or hill;
Ne'er saw I, never felt, a calm so deep!
The river glideth at his own sweet will:
Dear God! The very houses seem asleep;
And all the mighty hearts lying still.

— Wordsworth, from "Composed upon
Westminster Bridge, September 3, 1802"

No, no, go not to Lethe, neither twist
    Wolfsbane, tight-rooted, for its poisonous wine;
Nor suffer thy pale forehead to be kissed
    By nightshade, ruby grape of Proserpine;
Make not your rosary of yew berries;
    Nor let the beetle, nor the death moth be
        Your mournful Psyche, nor the downy owl
A partner in your sorrow's mysteries.

— Keats, from "Ode on Melancholy"

Tears, idle tears, I know not what they mean,
Tears from the depth of some divine despair
Rise in the heart, and gather in the eyes,
In looking on the happy Autumn-fields,
And thinking of the days that are no more.

— Tennyson, from "Tears, idle tears"

With farmer Allan at the farm abode
William and Dora. William was his son,
And she his niece. He often looks at them,

And often thought, "I'll make them man and wife."
Now Dora felt her uncle's will in all,
And yearn'd toward William; but the youth, because
He had been always with her in the house,
Thought not of Dora.

— Tennyson, from "Dora"

Life, how and what is it? As here I lie
In this state-chamber, dying by degrees,
Hours and long hours in the dead night, I ask
'Do I live, am I dead?' Peace, peace seems all.
Saint Praxed's ever was the church for peace;
And so, about this tomb of mine. I fought
With tooth and nail to save my niche, ye know.

— Browning, from "The Bishop Orders His
Tomb at Saint Praxed's Church"

Well, I showed Arthur Amy signs enough
Off from the house as far we could keep
And from barn smells you can't wash out of ploughed ground
With all the rain and snow of seven years;
And I don't mean just skulls of Rogers' Rangers
On Moosilauke, but woman signs to man,
Only bewitched so I would last him longer.
Up where the trees grow short, the mosses tall,
I made him gather me wet snow berries
On slippery rocks beside a waterfall.
I made him do it for me in the dark.
And he liked everything I made him do.
I hope if he is where he sees me now
He's so far off he can't see what I've come to.
You *can* come down from everything to nothing.
All is, if I'd a-known when I was young
And full of it, that this would be the end,
It doesn't seem as if I'd had the courage
To make so free and kick up in folks' faces.
I might have, but it doesn't seem as if.

— Frost, from "A Servant to Servants"

Divinity must live within herself:
Passions of rain, or moods in falling snow;
Grievings in loneliness, or unsubdued
Emotions on wet roads on autumn nights;
All pleasures and all pains, remembering
The bough of summer and the winter branch.
These are the measures destined for the soul.

— Stevens, from "Sunday Morning"

Still on the bedroom wall, the list of rules.
Don't waste the water. It is pumped by hand.
Don't throw old blades into the W.C.
Don't keep the bathroom long and don't be late
For meals and don't hang swim-suits out on sills
(A line has been provided at the back). .
Don't empty children's sand-shoes in the hall.
Don't this, Don't that. Ah, still the same, the same
As it was last year and the year before—
But rather more expensive now, of course.

— John Betjeman, from "Beside the Seaside"

The sun is blue and scarlet on the page,
And *yuck-a, yuck-a, yuck-a, yuck-a,* rage
The yellowhammers mating. Yellow fire
Blankets the captives dancing on their pyre,
And the scorched lector screams and drops his rod.
Trojans are singing to their drunken God,
Ares. Their helmets catch on fire. Their files
Clank by the body of my comrade—miles
Of filings! Now the scythe-wheeled chariot rolls
Before their lances long as vaulting-poles.

— R. Lowell, from "Falling Asleep Over the Aeneid"

Then priestly sanction, then the drop of sound.
Quickly part to the cavern ever warm
deep from the march, body to body bound,

descend (my soul) out of dismantling storm
into the darkness where the world is made.
... Come back to the bright air. Love is multiform.

— J. Berryman, from "Canto Amor"

Another voice drowns out Miss McIntosh.
It's Mel Torme, singing *Who's Sorry Now?*
Followed by a Kid Ory version of
Quincy Street Stomp, and bringing back in view
The bright upholstery of the present tense,
The lax geography of pillows, gin-
And-bitters with anesthetic bitterness.
It must be three AM, but never mind.
Open upon her lap lies *The New Yorker*.

— Anthony Hecht, from "The Short End"

Green-shadowed people sit, or walk in rings,
Their children finger the awakened grass,
Calmly a cloud stands, calmly a bird sings,
And, flashing like a dangled looking-glass,
Sun lights the balls that bounce, the dogs that bark,
The branch-arrested mist of leaf, and me,

— Philip Larkin, from "Spring"

Bind us in time, O Seasons clear, and awe.
O minstrel galleons of Carob fire,
Bequeath us to no earthly shore until
Is answered in the vortex of our grave
The seal's wide spindrift gaze toward paradise.

— Hart Crane, from "Voyages"

EXAMPLES OF THE 4-FOOT LINE:

Wouldst thou hear what man can say
In a little? Reader, stay.
Underneath this stone doth lie
As much beauty as could die;
To more virtue than doth live.
If at all she had a fault,
Leave it buried in this vault.
One name was Elizabeth;
Th'other, let it sleep with death:
Fitter, where it died, to tell,
Than that it lived at all. Farewell.

> — Ben Jonson, from "Epitaph on Elizabeth, L.H."

What wond'rous Life is this I lead!
Ripe Apples drop about my head;
The Luscious Clusters of the Vine
Upon my Mouth do crush their Wine;
The Nectarine, and curious Peach,
Into my hands themselves do reach;
Stumbling on Melons, as I pass,
Ensnar'd with Flow'rs, I fall on Grass.
Meanwhile the Mind, from pleasure less,
Withdraws into its happiness:
The Mind, that Ocean where each kind
Does straight its own resemblance find;
Yet it creates, transcending these
Far other Worlds, and other Seas;
Annihilating all that's made
To a green thought in a green shade

> — Andrew Marvell, from "The Garden"

While the cock with lively din,
Scatters the rear of darkness thin,
And to the stack, or the barn door,
Stoutly struts his dames before;

Oft listening how the hounds and horn
Cheerly rouse the slumbering morn,
From the side of some oar hill,
Through the high wood echoing shrill.

— Milton, from "L'Allegro"

No nightingale did ever chant
More welcome notes to weary bands
of travellers in some shady haunt
Among Arabian sands:
A voice so thrilling ne'er was heard
In springtime from the cuckoo-bird,
Breaking the silence of the seas
Among the farthest Hebrides.

—Wordsworth, from "The Solitary Reaper"

No more with overflowing light
Shall fill the eyes that now are faded,
Nor shall another's fringe with night
Their woman-hidden world as they did.
No more shall quiver down the days
The flowing wonder of her ways,
Whereof no language may requite
The shifting and the many-shaded.

— E. A. Robinson, from "For a Dead Lady"

That night your great guns, unawares,
Shook all our coffins as we lay,
And broke the chancel window-squares,
We thought it was the Judgment-day...

Again the guns disturbed the hour,
Roaring their readiness to avenue,
As far inland as Stourton Tower,
And Camelot, and starlit Stonehenge.

—Thomas Hardy, from "Channel Firing"

Earth, receive an honoured guest;
William Yeats is laid to rest:
Let the Irish vessel lie
Emptied of its poetry.

In the nightmare of the dark
All the dogs of Europe bark,
And the living nations wait
Each sequestered in its hate.

—Auden, from "In Memory of W.B. Yeats"

COMMENTS

The monotonous repetition of special sequences of balanced contours in evenly spaced Rhythm units—especially if it causes normal grammatical units to be broken up—produces SINGSONG. One such sequence is [the intonation pattern usually used in a Mother Goose rhyme like Mary had a little lamb]; it may be said to have the meaning of RECITAL.

— Kenneth L. Pike, from *The Intonation of American English*

These mountains witnesse shall, so shall these vallies,
These forrests eke, made wretched by our musique,
Our morning hymne is this, and song at evening.

The language itself makes it clear that this is no ordinary speech, but something more like Incantation. It requires the special effects that are the metrical pattern here, or would have to say with its intonation, This is a very special way of talking. When the language is this far removed from the ordinary uses, the intonation suggested by the metrical pattern is probably as good as any. At least it has slight competition.

—Thompson, from *The Founding of English Metre*

[English poets of the mid-16th century] got what they wanted, a steady progression of alternate stresses which tends always to cause the stress-patterns of speech and the patterns of metre to become one. But when the patterns become one, the words lack a real intonation and so lack the best part of that indication of feeling which is tone.

—Thompson, from *The Founding of English Metre*

It remains true that much of the verse written in the fifteenth and early sixteenth centuries is difficult to rhythmize with any satisfaction. I think that during the transition to the Elizabethan mode of smoothly flowing metre some of the clumsy rhythms may have resulted from a conception that a verse line consisted essentially in a fixed number of syllables, without regard to patterns of differentiated stress. This complicating conception may have been especially influential in translations. Wyatt's sonnets, modeled on Italian poems, have many lines of this kind, with the syllabic count (of ten or twelve) scrupulously observed but the rhythmical patterns apparently given second place, for instance:

Sigh then no more, syns no way man may fined
Thy virtue to let, though that frowerdnes
Of fortune me holdeth; and yet, as I may gesso,
Though other be present, thou are not all behinde.

— D.W. Harding, from *Words into Rhythm*

Occasionally there may be some hesitation over small points, but such uncertainties don't matter very much because they can be resolved either way without harm. For example, this line in Shakespeare's Sonnet 30: "And with old woes new waile my deare times waste" is clearly (as we know anyway from its occurrence in a sonnet) an iambic pentameter, and good metrical sense is made by simply marking off five regular iambic feet. But one may hesitate, perhaps, over the first foot: a reading of these two rather unemphatic words with greater stress on the first is at least equally possible, to give a reversed foot.

One must simply choose which reading one prefers. A good rule in such cases is to prefer the scansion that most nearly fulfills the regular pattern of expectation.

— James McAuley, from *Versification*

Many examples could be quoted of the play that poets make with the first syllable while keeping to an iambic pattern:

Shut, shut the door, good John! fatigu'd, I said (Pope)

Once—never mind where, how, why, when,—once say (Browning)

> they on the trading flood
> Through the wide Ethiopian to the Cape
> Ply stemming nightly towards the Pole. (Milton)

— McAuley, from *Versification*

Once we recognize that equality of stress is the limit-case which still satisfies the metre, there should be no difficulty. Where the stress values are equal, metrical values are assigned in accordance with metrical expectation: an equal-stress foot in an iambic line is iambic, but trochaic in a trochaic line. To do otherwise than this is to invite confusion and uncertainty, and break down the distinction between metre and stress which we have labored to establish. It would certainly be a misreading of our experience; for, when the metre tells us to expect an iamb, what we experience in an equal-stress foot is an iamb, though one in which the relation between the syllables has been brought to the limit position. So in Donne's line:

All kings and all their favorites

the point about the first foot is that it is an iamb, in which for logical and rhetorical reasons the unaccented syllable has been brought up into as much prominence as it can have without reversing the foot.

— McAuley, from *Versification*

When pitch becomes expressively significant in verse, it is usually hard to disentangle the effect of pitch from the other two features mentioned, duration and phonetic quality.

— McAuley, from *Versification*

I understand your meanyng by your eye.
Your meaning I understand by your eye.

In these two verses there seemth no difference at all, since the one hath the very self same words that the other hath, and yet the latter verse is neyther true nor pleasant, and the first verse may

94

passe the musters. The fault of the latter verse is that this worde
understand is therein so placed as the grave accent falleth upon *der*,
and thereby maketh *der*, in this worde *understand* to be elevated:
which is contrarie to the naturall or usuall pronunciation: for we
say *understand*, and not *understand*.

— George Gascoigne, from *Notes of Instruction*
Concerning the Making of English Verse

Sigh no more, ladies, sigh no more

...lends itself to varied emphasis of the repeated phrase, which
the iambic base suggests, though it does not compel it. The
wisdom of preferring, other things being equal, the more regular
of any two possible metrical readings may perhaps be reinforced
by (this example) of how the ignoring of the iambic base may
result in our overlooking an interesting reading.

— McAuley, from *Versification*

Milton is bold in his metric, but his conscience is exacting, and
his irregularities come under the the conventions. He writes:

Weep no more, woe ful Shep herds, weep no more,

The brilliance of this line consists in its falling eventually,
and after we have tried other readings in vain, into the entire
regularity which was the last thing we expected of it. We are used
to receiving the impression, which he likes to give, and which
represents a part of the truth, that his determinate meaning
produces an indeterminateness in the local meters of nearly
every line, even if we understand that this indeterminateness
stops at the limits of the permissive convention. Under that
impression we were inclined to scan the line this way:

Weep no more, woe ful Shep herds, weep no more,

which is a metrical line found many times in Milton; but we
were troubled over what happened to the logic of the accentless
woeful. We said to ourselves, however, that the first *weep no more*

had precisely the same logical values as the second one. All the same, the *woeful* is really not up to Milton's level as a workman, and we are not content with it. We finally try the normal meter, and we see that Milton intended us to come to it, and thought we must come to it if we believed in his technical competence. In the phrase *weep no more* it is difficult to say that one word has a heavier logical accent than another; yet we cannot accent them all, as we should like to do, and would do in prose. Or can we? The fact is that, reading the line as we finally do, we not only accent all three words but are obliged to: first *no*, then *weep*, then *more*; for the phrase occurs twice. Again the meter is informative. It could not be so if there were not the most minute give-and-take between the meaning and the meter as principles trying to determine each other, and arriving every moment or so at peace with honor, which means careful adjustments by means of reciprocal concessions.

– John Crowe Ransom, from *The New Criticism*

Isochronism is felt, not 'real.' Meter releases rhythmic potential; it creates an illusion of time, not a chronometric interval. If we measure the feet in the example from Hart Crane (The River, spreading, flows—and spends your dream.), we can show significant differences in actual length. But we have the illusion that the feet occupy units of equal time because the total effect of metrical organization seemingly eliminates temporal discrepancies. Meter is analogous to perspective. If we measure with a ruler the distance between Mona Lisa's nose and her fingertips, and between her nose and one of the rocks she sits among, we may conclude that it is no farther from her nose to her hand than it is from her nose to an imagined point two or three hundred yards distant. What we measure with our ruler is literal space on canvas, not the illusion of space created by illusory time. That meter also occupies literal time—the minutes elapsing as we read a poem—is irrelevant just as the measurable dimensions of a painting in perspective are irrelevant.

– Harvey Gross, from *Sound and Form in Modern Poetry*

FURTHER EXAMPLES AND 'TEST' LINES AND PASSSAGES:

1)a   Faithless, forsworn, thy dame ne goddess was,
            Nor Darden's beginner of thy race,
            But of hard rocks Mount Caucasia monstruous
            Bred thee, and teats of tiger gave thee suck.

                                      (Surrey: early 16th century)

    b   Thy mother was no goddess, perjur'd man,
            Nor Darden's the author of thy stock;
            But thou art sprung from Scythian Caucasus,
            And tigers of Hernia gave thee suck.

                              (Marlowe, late 16th century)

2)a   And swims or sinks, or wades, or creeps, or flyes.
    b   With head, hands, wings, or feet pursues his way.
    c   And ten low words oft creep in one dull line.
    d   A Mr. Wilkinson, a clerygyman.
    e   Or spirit of the nethermost Abyss.
    f   Than tired eyelids upon tired eyes.
    g   Bless ye the nosegay in the vale.

Vladimir Nabokov on prosody (Appendix Two of Volume III of his translation of Pushkin's EUGENE ONEGIN—pp 452-4):

The samples given below illustrate the five combinations (of one ictus and one or two depressions) mathematically possible within the limits of one metrical foot. The first two are masculine tetrameters: 1) iambic and 2) trochaic; the rest are masculine tetrameters: dactylic, 4) amphibrachic, and 5) anapestic.

The rós- | es are | agáin | in blóom
Róses | are a- | gáin in | blóom
Róses a- | gáin are in | blóom
The róses | agáin are | in blóom
And the rós- | es agáin | are in blóom

An example of pausative or cadential verse using the same words would run:

And again the rose is in bloom

which the metrically trained ear hears as three anapests with one missed depression in the second foot causing a little gasp or pause, hence the term.

And a syllable line would be:

De nouveau la rose fleurit

In which the *e* or *rose* is a type of depression that cannot be rendered in English, German or Russian. An iambic foot cannot be illustrated by a word unless that word is part of a specific iambic line. An iambic foot can be illustrated by signs only insofar as those signs are made to express the maximal four variations in which an iambic foot actually appears in verse:

˘ ´ regular beat	˘ - scud
˘ - tilted scud (or false trochee)	˘ ´ false spondee

To the discussion of these we shall now turn.

An ordinary iambic foot (i.e., one not affected by certain contractional and rhymal variations) consists of two semeia, the first tractional and rhymal variations) consists of two semeia, the first semiion being called a depression (˘ or ˘) and the second an ictus (- or ´). Any such foot belongs to one of the following types (with the basic metrical stress marked -, and the variable word accent ´):

1) Regular foot, ˘ ´ (unaccented nonstress followed by accented stress); e.g., "Appease my grief, and deadly pain" (Surrey)

2) Scudded foot (or false pyrrhic), ˘ - (unaccented nonstress followed by unaccented stress); e.g., "In expectation of a guest" (Tennyson)

3) Tilt (or inversion), ◡́ - (accented nonstress followed by unaccented stress); e.g., "Vaster than empires and more slow" (Marvell)

4) False spondee, ◡́ -́ (accented nonstress and accented stress); e.g., "Twice holy was the Sabbath-bell" (Keats).

[note: examples abridged]

SOUND AND SENSE

Sound can resemble nothing but sound.

— Dr. Johnson, from *The Rambler*

The music of poetry is not something which exists apart from the meaning.

—T.S. Eliot, from "The Music of Poetry"

Syllables and words, even elementary phrases, are language units which phonetically have very little more color of their own than chameleons. The character which they take on so instantly and display so positively is that of the logical meanings. (Central or marginal, denotative or connotative meanings.) The phonetic elements would not be serviceable for language if they were not indefinitely negotiable; that is, able to be dissociated quickly and cleanly from given meanings and reassociated with fresh ones. But many critics, especially if they are not themselves composers, confuse cause and effect. The poetic image, let us say, is of green grass, and not vice versa as ignorant persons suppose. The critics do not see how modest are the limits within which poets seek rhythm, which should not be at all foreign to the common genius of the language, and some degree of euphony, which is easily obtained, and otherwise have no great concern with phonetic projects.

. . . With the many *f*'s and *r*'s and *th*'s a fine feeling of fluffiness
is given to one line by the many unaccented syllables:

Comfort, softer than the feathers of its breast,
Sounds as soft as the bird's downy breast feels . . .

the cause is said to be the many unaccented syllables, assisted by the many *f*'s, *r*'s, and *th*'s. But I will substitute a line which preserves all these factors and departs from the given line mainly by rearrangement:

Crumpets for the foster-fathers of the brats.
Here I miss the fluffiness and the downiness.

– John Crowe Ransom, from "The Poet as a Woman"

…the metre in itself does not carry these expressive powers: it has a potentiality which is actualized and specified only by the words: it absorbs the mood of the words, but in turn supports and enhances that mood.

– James McAuley, from *A Primer of English Versification*

In thus speaking of the expressive, as well as the musical, value of speech-sounds, I have avoided any suggestion that these things exist to any important degree apart from the meaning. It is only through the meaning that the expressive potential of speech-sounds is actually released: sounds respond to and co-operate with the sense. This is also true, to a large extent, of the "musical" quality of verse. While it is too extreme to say, as some critics have done, that words can have no "musical" value apart from the meaning—one can, for instance, makes nonsense verses that are mellifluous or rhythmically and phonetically interesting—it must be admitted that the musicality we admire is a mainly the result of an interaction between sense and sound: meaning is the prince that kisses the sleeping beauty of speech-sound into wakeful life. It should also be added that in a discussion of this sort one tends to choose examples of the most obvious kind, with sound supporting the sense in an easily demonstrable way. But the art of the poet is not confined to such specific and demonstrable effects (which can degenerate into mere tricks); it is shown above all in a general mating of words and meaning to produce life, energy, and delight, as the physical body of verse sings and dances while incarnating the theme.

Probably it is the rhythm of poetry which is its most definitive feature. We may leave aside the usual natural analogies, although for some these provide a warrant for the appearance and almost mystical significance of rhythm in poetry—the cycles of the seasons, the tides, even the blood-pulse and the process of breathing, all of which are, indeed, in their various ways and at various paces, rhythmical; however suggestive, they seem to me, except perhaps for the analogy to breathing, fairly remote. All successions of spoken words necessarily have a rhythm of sorts, and the rhythm of poetry has a natural enough warrant in this alone, for its rhythm is only the rhythm of speech—or prose—more highly organized and therefore presumable more notable. Its rhythm is not only a significant aspect of the formal character of a poem, continually insisting as it does on the fact that the materials of the poem are not haphazardly there but are the result of an at least partially willed arrangement; rhythm is not only one of the significant means by which special attention is called to the words of a poem, insinuating as it does their sound-values into our consciousness (beyond whatever aptness the words may bear to the plain sense or argument of the poem) and moreover placing and binding them together in a context that is not merely syntactical: the rhythm exists for these purposes, certainly, but for its own sake as well. And all this is true, more or less, whether the poem is written in the traditional meters or in free verse, whether the "music" of the poem approaches the one extreme of song or the other extreme of speech. It has often been suggested that the meters serve to reinforce by their appropriateness the subject of the poem, that is, to imitate somehow: so in Browning's "How They Brought the Good News from Ghent to Aix" the trisylabic meters gallop as the horses theoretically do, with a sort of desperate kuh-klopety-klop, and there is a famous passage in Pope's "An Essay of Criticism" which means to illustrate this way of thinking:

> Soft is the strain when Zephyr gently blows,
> And the smooth stream in smoother numbers flows:
> But when loud surges lash the sounding shore,
> The hoarse, rough verse should like the torrent roar:
> When Ajax strives some rock's vast weight to throw,
> The line too labors, and the words move slow;
> Not so, when swift Camilla scours the plain,
> Flies o'er th'unbending corn, and skims along the main.

On the other hand, any imitation so direct is likely to seem primitive or naïve, and John Crowe Ransom suggested that what the meters imitate is nothing less than an abstraction, a sort of Platonic universal—which is perhaps to say somewhat grandly and speculatively only that the meters operate with less realism than does the argument or "plot" of the poem; in other words, the meters can and do exist as an object of interest apart from the paraphrasable meaning of the poem and are therefore capable of their own perfections without respect to their possible function in following sense.

Even the meters—so it seems to me can imitate only by convention. Let take a simple case. Yvor Winters once offered his line, "The slow cry of a bird," as an example of metrical imitation, not strictly as he put it, of the birdcall itself but of "the slowness of the cry." The convention would seem to be that two or more strong syllables in succession carry associations of slowness and heaviness, while two or more weak syllables in succession carry contrary associations of rapidity and lightness: melancholy on the one hand, playfulness on the other. But the displacement of a stress from *of* to *cry* in the Winters line, bringing two stresses together, fails to slow the line down, as I hear it. Substitute for this "The quick cry of a bird," and the two weak syllables following cry can be said to do as much to speed the line up, or as little. But whether the cry is to sound quick or slow, the metrical situation remains, practically speaking, identical. If any question of interpretation arises from the reversed foot, the meaning of the reversal must depend on the denotation of the adjective rather than on the particular arrangement of syllables and stresses, for denotation overrides any implication of the meters apart from it. Though apparently agreed on by generations of poets (or perhaps only critics), the minor convention on which Winters was depending is hardly observed any longer except in criticism or occasionally the classroom. Nor was it, for that matter, observed by Milton in his great melancholy-playful air, "Il Penseroso" and "L'Allegro," or if observed, than only to be consciously played against. Composers of music for the movies learned early that direct imitation of a visual image through sound was best restricted to comic effects (pizzicati, trombone glissandi, staccato bassoons). Pushed far enough, and that is not very far at all, the results of metrical imitation can seem similarly cartoonlike:

> I sank to the pillow, and Joris, and he;
> I slumbered, Dirck slumbered, we slumbered all three.

In any case, simple imitation by means of rhythm would seem to be more plausible in free verse, with its greater flexibility, and most workable in prose, which is allowed any and every arrangement of syllables. And yet I have seen nowhere any critical offering to this effect.

If the meters do represent or imitate anything in general, it may be nothing more (or less) than some psychological compulsion, a sort of counting on the fingers or stepping on the cracks, magic to keep an unpredictable world under control.

(from "Meters and Memory")

SONG

Let us begin with the difference between musical rhythm, in any style of music, and verse rhythm, in any language. In music a difference in temporal duration between two notes is more noticeable than a difference in accentuation; musical "prosody", so to speak, is always quantitative, not qualitative, and in a much stricter way than any spoken verse can be which, like Greek or classical Latin, is scanned quantitatively. If in quantitative scansion syllables are classified as either long or short, every long syllable being temporally equivalent to two short syllables, this classification, when applied to a spoken language, is, strictly speaking, a fiction, for probably no two spoken syllables are exactly the same length. But in music, for any given metronome marking, all quarter notes, say, are identical in duration. Also, instead of there being only two kinds of lengths, there are infinite possibilities of sustaining and dividing notes. When, therefore, a line of verse in any language, no matter what its prosodic principle, is sung, the rhythm the ear perceives is based on differences in length. Differences in accent are also often perceptible, but they are always secondary. Further, the ear's judgment of tempo when hearing music is quite different when hearing speech: a tempo of spoken syllables which feels like an adagio would, if the syllables were musical notes, feel like an allegretto.

When poets discover that their language is most easily organized rhythmically by using certain kinds of feet and certain kinds of meters, they tend to fall into the habit of using these exclusively, as if no other kinds were possible. To this habit, a familiarity with the art of vocal music can be a valuable corrective. For, while listening to a song, the verses of which were written, say, in iambics, one hears not only iambics, but any number of other feet, amphibrachs, cretics, tribrachs, spondees, etc., which can suggest to the poet all kinds of rhythmical possibilities for spoken verse. This is particularly true, perhaps, in the case of English, owing to its large number of monosyllabic words, the metrical value of which is not innate but depends on their position in the line. In a language like German, for example, which has an accentual prosody and many polysyllabic words, metrical innovations are much more difficult, for one polysyllabic word in a line can dictate the meter of the rest of the words in it.

If the lyrics of the Elizabethan poets are rhythmically more interesting than those of other periods, it is difficult to escape the conclusion that the close association of poets with musicians of high caliber was largely responsible.

Dryden and Burns are excellent song writers, but their songs have a metrical conventionality from which the Elizabethans were free; and it is to be noticed that those Romantic lyrics which are most exciting rhythmically, like some of Blake's and Beddoes', are consciously modeled on the Elizabethans. The normal conventions of spoken English verse make small provision for monosyllabic feet or for the spondee, and frown on changes of metrical base within a stanza. In these songs we find such things constantly, and very effective they sound when only spoken, e.g.:

Deare, sweet, faire, wise, change, shrinke nor be not weake

Not a friend, not a friend greet
My poor corpse, where my bones shall be thrown.
> A thousand thousand sighs to save, lay me o where
> Sad true lover never find my grave, to weep there.

— Auden, from his introduction to An Elizabethan Song Book
[additional stanzas and musical notation added by Donald Justice]

COMMENT

Compare:

Fly away, fly away, breath,
I am slain by a fair cruel maid.
My shroud of white, struck all with yew, O prepare it!
My part of death, no one so true did share it.

Compare:

But if you let your lovers mone,
The Faerie Queene Proserpina,
Will send abroad her Fairies ev'ry one,
That shall pinch blacke and blew,
Your white hands, and faire armes,
That did not kindly rue
Your Paramours harmes.

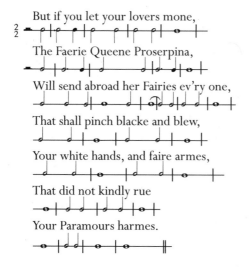

Compare:

All you that love, or lov'd before,
The Faerie Queene Proserpina
Bids you encrease that loving humour more,
They that yet have not fed
On delight amourous,
She vowes that they shall lead
Apes in Avernus.

Such lines have indeed, as Saintsbury declares, their own vocal music, but their authors would not have found it, had they not been writing songs.

Though words take time to say, as notes take time to play, words do not, as notes do, express their meanings as well. In music, that is, the movement is the expression; in poetry it is but a very small part of it. The elements of the poetic vocabulary, therefore, which are best adapted for musical setting are those which requires the least reflection to comprehend—its most dynamic and its most immediate. For example: interjections, which in one's mother tongue always sound onomatopoeic (fie, O, alas, adieu); imperatives; verbs of physical motion (going, coming, hasting, following, falling) or physical concomitants of emotions (laughing, weeping, frowning, sighing); adjectives denoting elementary qualities (bright, hard, green, sad); nouns denoting states of feeling (joy, love, rage, despair) or objects, the emotional associations of which are common to all, and strong (sea, night, moon, spring). On the other hand, complicated metaphors which, even if the words are heard, take time to understand and didactic messages which demand assent or dissent are unsuitable. Again, since music, generally speaking, can express only one thing at a time, it is ill adapted to verses which express mixed or ambiguous feelings, and prefers poems which either express one emotional state or successively contrast two states. Lastly, since words take much longer to sing than to speak, even without the repetitions that music so often requires, poems intended for songs must be short. Ballads and epic chants, in which the music is a subordinate carrier for the words, are another matter.

    — Auden, from his introduction to *An Elizabethan Song Book* [additional stanzas and musical notation added by Donald Justice]

Compare further:

Hark al you ladies do sleep,
The fairy queen Prosperina
Bids you awake and pitie them that weep,
You may doe in the dark

What the day doth forbid,
Feare not the dogs that barke,
Night will have all hid.

But if you let your lovers mone...

In Myrtle Arbours on the downes,
The Fairie Queen Prosperina,
This night by moone-shine leading merrie rounds,
Holds a watch with sweet love,
Down the dale, up the hill,
No plaints or groanes may move
Their holy vigill.

All you that will hold watch with love,
The Fairie Queen Prosperina,
Will make you fairer than Diones dove,
Roses red, Lillies white
And the clear damaske hue
Shall on your cheeks alight,
Love will adorne you.

All you that love, or lov'd before...

—Thomas Campion, from "Hark, All You Ladies"

METRICAL EXAMPLES

Sing, cucco, nu. Sing, cuccu.
Sing, cucco. Sing, cuccu, nu.

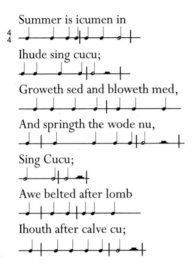

Summer is icumen in

Ihude sing cucu;

Groweth sed and bloweth med,

And springth the wode nu,

Sing Cucu;

Awe belted after lomb

Ihouth after calve cu;

Bulloc sterteth, bucke verteth,

Murie sing Cucu.

Cucu, Cucu,

Wel singes thu Cucu,

Ne swik thu naver nu.

— Anonymous

Weep no more, sad fountains
What need you flow so fast?
Look how the snowy mountains
Heaven's the sun doth gently waste
But my sun's heavenly eyes
View not your weeping
That now lie sleeping
Softly, now softly lies
Sleeping.

Sleep is a reconciling,
A rest that peace begets.
Doth not the sun rise smiling
When fair at even he sets?
Rest you then rest, sad eyes,
Melt not in weeping

While she lies sleeping
Softly, now softly lies
Sleeping.

— Anonymous

Come away, come away, death,
And in sad cypress let me be laid
Fly away, fly away, breath
I am slain by a fair cruel maid.
My shroud of white, stuck all with yew,
O, prepare it!
My part of death, no one so true
Did share it.

Not a flower, not a flower sweet,
On my black coffin let there be strown
Not a friend, not a friend greet
My poor corpse where my bones shall be
A thousand sighs to save, thrown.
Lay me, O, where
Sad true lover never find my grave,
To weep there.

— Shakespeare, from *Twelfth Night* (Act II, Scene IV)

Under the greenwood tree
Who loves to lie with me
And turn his merry note
Unto the sweet bird's throat
Come hither, come hither, come hither:
Here shall he see
No enemy
But winter and rough weather.

Who doth ambition shun
And loves to live i' the sun,
Seeking the food he eats,
And pleased with what he gets,
Come hither, come hither, come hither:

Here shall he see
No enemy
But winter and rough weather.

— Shakespeare, from *As You Like It* (Act II Scene V)

When the rye reach to the chin,
And chopcherry, chopcherry ripe within,
Strawberries swimming in the cream,
And schoolboys playing in the stream;
Then O, then O, my true love said,
She could not live a maid.

— George Peele, from "When the rye reach to the chin"

Hot sun, cool fire, tempered with sweet air,
Black shade, fair nurse, shadow my white hair.
Shine, sun; burn, fire; breathe, air, and ease me;
Black shade, fair nurse, shroud me and please me.
Shadow, my sweet nurse, keep me from burning;
Make not my glad cause cause of mourning.
      Let not my beauty's fire
      Inflame unstaid desire,
      Nor pierce any bright eye
      That wandered lightly.

— George Peele, from "Hot Sun, Cool Fire"

Slow, slow, fresh fount, keeper time with my salt teares;
Yet slower, yet, o faintly gentle springs:
List to the heavy part the musique beares,
  "Woe weepes out her division, when shee sings.
  Drupe hearbs, and flowers,
  Fall griefe in showers;
  Our beauties are not ours:
          O, I could still

(Like melting snow upon some craggier hill,)
  drop, drop, drop, drop,
Since natures pride is, now, a wither's Daffodill.

> – Ben Jonson, from "The Masque of the Gypsies"

A cypress-bough, and a rose-wreathswet,
  A wedding-robe, and a winding-sheet,
    A bridal bed and a bier.
  Thine be the kisses, maid,
      And smiling Love's alarms;
  And thou, pale youth, be laid
      In the grave's cold arms.
    Each in his own charms.
        Death and Hymen both are here;
          So up with scythe and torch,
          And to the old church porch,
      While all the bells ring clear:
    And rosy, rosy the bed shall bloom,
    And earthy, earthy heap up the tomb.

> –Thomas Lovell Beddoes, from "Bridal Song and Dirge"

That the topless towers be burnt
And men recall that face,
Move most gently if move you must
In this lonely place.
She thinks, part woman, three parts a child,
That nobody looks; her feet
Practise a tinker shuffle
Picked up on a street.
Like a long-legged fly upon the stream
Her mind moves upon silences.

> –Yeats, from "Long Legged Fly"

Deftly, admiral, cast your fly
  Into the slow deep hover,
    Till the wise old trout mistake and die;
      Salt are the deeps that cover

The glittering flets you led,
   White is your head.

   Read on, ambassador, engrossed
In your favorite Stendhal;
   The Outer Provinces are lost,
Unshaven horsemen swill
The great wines of the Chateaux
   Where you danced long ago...

                —W. H. Auden, from "Five Songs"

You're nobody's sweetheart now.
They don't baby you somehow.
You're out of place in your own home town.
   Fancy hose, silken gown,
   You're out of place in your own home town.
When you walk down the Avenue,
I just can't believe it's you.
   Painted lips, painted eyes
   Wearing a bird of Paradise.
It all seems wrong somehow,
You're nobody's sweetheart now.

— Gustav Kahn and Ernie Erdman, from "Nobody's Sweetheart Now"

It was just one of those things,
Just one of those crazy flings,
One of those bells that now and then rings
   Just one of those things.

It was just one of those nights,
Just one of those fabulous flights,
A trip to the moon on gossamer wings,
   Just one of those things...

        —Cole Porter, from "Just One of Those Things"

Do, do, do
What you've done, done, done

    Before, Baby.
Do, do, do
What I do, do, do
    Adore, Baby.

Let's try again,
Sigh again,
Fly again
        to heaven.
Baby, see
It's A B C—
I love you and you love me.

                    — Ira Gershwin, from "Do, Do,Do"

Early this morning when you knocked upon my door,
Early this morning when you knocked upon my door,
And I said, "Hello, Satan, I believe it's time to go…"

                — Robert Johnson, from "Me and the Devil Blues"

EXAMPLES OF SONG-LIKE STANZAS
IN POEMS OF OTHER TYPES:

Go and catch a falling star,
Get with child a mandrake root,
Tell me where all past years are,
Or who cleft the Devil's foot,
Teach me to hear mermaids singing,
Or to keep off envy's stinging,
        And find
        What wind
Serves to advance an honest mind.

If thou be'st born to strange sights,
Things invisible to see,
Ride ten thousand days and nights,
Till age snow white hairs on thee.
Thou, when thou return'st will tell me
All strange wonders that befell thee,
        And swear
        Nowhere
Lives a woman true, and fair.

If thou find'st one, let me know,
Such a pilgrimage were sweet;
Yet do not, I would not go,
Though at next door we might meet;
Though she were true when you met her,
And last till you write your letter,
        Yet she
        Will be
False, ere I come, to two, or three.

— John Donne, from "Song"

The trumpet's loud clangor
  Excites us to arms,
With shrill notes of anger
  And mortal alarms.

The double double double beat
  Of the thundering drum
  Cries "hark! The foes come;
Charge, charge! 'til too late to retreat!"

The soft complaining flute
  In dying notes discovers
  The woes of hopeless lovers,
Whose dirge is whispered by the warbling lute....

        – John Dryden, from "A Song for St. Cecilia's Day"

The Rainbow comes and goes
  And lovely is the Rose,
  The Moon doth with delight
  Look round her when the heavens are bare,
        Waters on a starry night
        Are beautiful and fair;
  The sunshine is a glorious birth;
  But yet I know wher'er I go,
That there hath past away a glory from the earth.

  O evil day! If I were sullen
  While Earth herself is adorning,
        This sweet May-morning,
  And the Children all culling
        On every side,
        In a thousand valleys far and wide,
  Fresh flowers; while the sun shines warm,
And the Babe leaps up on his mother's arm:——
  I hear, I hear, with joy I hear!
  ——But there's a Tree, of many, one,
A single Field which I have looked upon,
Both of them speak of something that is gone:
  The pansy at my feet
  Doth the same tale repeat:
Whither is fled the visionary gleam?
Where is it now, the glory and the dream?

        – William Wordsworth, from "Ode"

FREE VERSE

Li Po [7th century] complained of the followers of C'u Yuan [writers of a sort of vers libber in Chinese] that they were writing "bubbles not waves."

– according to Pound

When this verse [Jerusalem] was first dictated to me, I consider'd a Monotonous Cadence, like that used by Milton & Shakespeare & all writers of English Blank Verse, derived from the modern bondage of Rhyming, to be a necessary and indispensible part of Verse. But I soon found that in the mouth of a true Orator such monotony was not only awkward, but as much a bandage as rhyme itself. I therefore have produced a variety in every line, both of cadences & number of syllables. Every word and every letter is studied and put into its fit place; the terrific numbers are reserved for the terrific parts, the mild & gentle for the mild & gentle parts, and the prosaic for inferior parts; all are necessary to each other. Poetry Fetter's Fetters the Human Race.

– William Blake, from *Jerusalem*

The form is mechanic, when on any given material we impress a pre-determined form, not necessarily arising out of the properties of the material;—as when to a mess of wet clay we give the shape we wish it to retain when hardened. The form is mechanic, when on any given material we impress a pre-determined form, not necessarily arising out of the properties of the material;—as when to a mess of wet clay we give the shape we wish it to retain when hardened.

— Samuel Taylor Coleridge, from *Complete Works*

There is one tangible result in poetry of the Symbolist effort; the break-up of the verse. French verse is no longer written as Sully Prudhomme wrote it. The caesura is abolished and only survives by chance or habit in view of a particular effect. An exact number of syllables is no longer necessary to the measure of the verse, the mutes count or not according to the musical design. Rich rhyme seems to belong to parody; no one takes this 'bijou d'un sou' seriously; to our ears, which are tired or too refined to enjoy brazen sound, verses à la Banville seem constructed upon laborious rhyme-endings. Even a simple assonance satisfies us better, and we are more charmed by the surprise produced by sounds that are slightly dissimilar than by the noisy concordance of cymbal-clashing rhymes. Finally the division of rhyme into masculine and feminine seems to us a puerile phonetic heresy; meurt and heure are excellent rhymes which will shock no one tomorrow. Parnassian versification is as far from us as Latin versification.

— Remy de Gourmont, from *Esthétique de la Langue Française*

Le vary vers libber est concu comme tel, c'est-dire comme fragment musical dessine sur le modele de son idée emotive, et non plus determine par la loi fixe du nombre.

— Remy de Gourmont (1899), from *Esthétique de la Langue Française*

I believe in an "absolute rhythm," that is, in poetry which corresponds exactly to the emotion or shade of emotion to be expressed. A man's rhythm must be interpretative, it will be, therefore, in the end, his own, uncounterfeiting, uncounterfeitable. [c 1912]

As regarding rhythm: to compose in the sequence of the musical phrase, not in sequence of a metronome. [March 1913]

Eliot has said the thing very well when he said, "No *vers* is *libber* for the man who wants to do a good job." [March 1913]

As a matter of details, there is vers libber with accent heavily marked as a drum-beat (as par example my "Dance Figure"), and on the other hand I think I have gone as far as can profitably be gone in the other direction (perhaps too far). I mean I do not think one can use to any advantage rhythms much more tenuous and imperceptible than some I have used. I think progress lies rather in an attempt to approximate classical quantitative metres (NOT to copy them) than in a carelessness regarding such things. [20 August, 1917]

— Ezra Pound, from "A Retrospect" and "A Few Don'ts"

Ideally each line of Howl is a single breath unit. Tho in this recording it's not pronounced so, I was exhausted at climax of 3 hour Chicago reading with Coors & Orlovsky. My breath is long—tee's the Measure, one physical-mental inspiration of thought contained in the elastic of a breath. It probably bugs Williams knows, but is a natural consequence, my own heightened conversation, not cooler average-dailytalk short breath. I got to mouth more madly this way. [1959]

A lot of these forms developed out of an extreme rhapsodic wail I once heard in a madhouse. [1959]

— Ginsberg, from *The New American Poetry* by Donald M. Allen

First writing on Kaddish was in Paris '58, several pages of part IV which set forth a new variation on the litany form used earlier in Howl—a graduated lengthening of the response lines, so that the Howl litany looks like a big pyramid on the page. Kaddish IV looks like three little pyramids sitting one on top of another, plus an upside-down pyramid mirror-reflected at that bottom of the series. Considered as breath, it means the vocal reader has to

121

build up the feeling-utterance three times to climax, and then, as coda, diminish the utterance to shorter and shorter sob. The first mess of composition had all these elements, I later cut it down to look neat and exact. [1966]

— Ginsberg, the jacket of Atlantic record number 4001

[Gustave Kahn] declared that his own free verse had developed out of experiments in poetic prose, in which he had attempted to interest Mallarmé before 1880. Characteristically, he explained the whole movement in the same way, contending that the new form proceeded from the poetic prose of the Romantics and the Parnassians, laying particular stress on the development of a conscious type of prose-poem from Aloisius Bertrand to Baudelaire. In one of Baudelaire's pieces, Les Bienfaits de la Lune, he thought the type had been realized to perfection. Some of his own prose-poems had appeared as early as 1879-80, before his departure on military service to Algeria. Returning to Paris in 1885, he took over La Vogue, one of the little reviews, which set out on its brief but illustrous course in April of the following year. The first of his vers libres to appear in print came in that review for 28 June 1886.

— P. Mansell Jones, concerning the history of the probable inventor of vers libre in French, from *The Background of Modern French Poetry: Essays and Interviews*

[The importance of Free Verse and particularly a sort of 'strophic' verse which Kahn devised] besides giving prominence to certain harmonies hitherto neglected, will be to enable every poet to realize his own type of verse, or rather an original strophe of his own, and to write an individual rhythm, instead of adopting a ready-made uniform which reduces him to being the pupil of some glorified predecessor or other.

— Gustave Kahn, from "Vogue"

And he speaks also of "un rythme absolument personnel."

L e vers libre ne mofifie pas, il ignore le nombre des syllables…
[It employs] une sort de pied rhythique superieur…[The old and new systems can be distinguished by the terms] vers syllabique and vers non-syllabiuque

— Eduard Dujardin

Vers libre has not even the excuse of a polemic; it is a battle-cry of freedom, and there is no freedom in art. And as the so-called vers libre which is good is anything but 'free,' it can better be defended under some other label. Particular types of vers libre may be supported on the choice of content, or on the method of handling the content. I am aware that many writers of vers libre have introduced such innovations, and that the novelty of their choice and manipulation of material is confused—if not in their own minds, in the minds of many of their readers—with the novelty of the form. But I am not here concerned with imagism, which is a theory about the use of material; I am only concerned with the theory of the verse-form in which imagism is cast. If vers libre is a genuine verse-form it will have a positive definition. And I can define it only in negatives: (1) absence of pattern, (2) absence of rhyme, (3) absence of metre.

But the most interesting verse which has yet been written in our language has been done either by taking a very simple form, like the iambic pentameter, and constantly withdrawing from it, or taking no form at all, and constantly approximating to a very simple one. It is this contrast between fixity and flux, this unperceived evasion of monotony, which is the very life of verse.

We may therefore formulate as follows: the ghost of some simple metre should lurk behind the arras in even the 'freest' verse; to advance menacingly as we doze, and withdraw as we rouse. Or, freedom is only truly freedom when it appears against the back-ground of an artificial limitation.

…and we conclude that the division between Conservative Verse and vers libre does not exist, for there is only good verse, bad verse, and chaos.

—T.S. Eliot (1917), from "Reflections on Vers Libre"

It would be convenient if poetry were always verse—either accented, alliterative, or quantitative; but that is not true. Poetry may occur, within a definite limit on one side, at any point along a line of which the formal limits are "verse" and "prose."

—T.S. Eliot (1932), from his preface to *Anabasis*

...at its leanest [free verse] still employs at least one technical device that is a characteristic of poetry and not of prose—the line...its rule is continual variation.

— Baum and Shapiro, from *A Prosody Handbook*

Free verse is a matter of degree. Just as accentual-syllabic verse with abundant disyllabic substitutions shades into accentual verse, so, if the number of stresses per line is not uniform or predictable, accentual verse shades into free verse. In the same way, as it leaves behind—like much contemporary poetry—the sense of the line as a strong element in the pattern, free verse shades into rhythmic prose.

Because in free verse the length of the line is determined by feel rather than established pattern, a crucial problem for the poet is knowing when to break lines...And two possibilities in the treatment of line-endings suggest two ultimate kinds of free verse. One kind, which John Hollander designates the oracular, exhibits unvarying line integrity, often with anaphora, as in Ginsberg's Howl or much of the formal Whitman...The effect is that of public speaking. But if constant enjambment takes place—that is, if the sense and syntax of one line run on into the next so that a hearer would have trouble ascertaining the line breaks—we have a very different kind of free verse, a kind we can designate as meditative and ruminative or private. It is this kind of vigorously enjambed free verse which has been a common style in the last twenty years or so.

One way the free-verse practitioner can exploit the device of varying from a norm is to offer a long line against a preceding grid of short ones, or a short line after we've got accustomed to long ones.

From these examples we can infer that a free-verse poem without dynamics—without, that is, perceptible interesting movement from one given to another or without significant variations from some more established by the texture of the poem—will risk the same sort of dullness as the metered poem which never varies from regularity. When it solicits our attention as poetry, a group of words arranged at apparent haphazard is as boring as tum-ti-tum.

A lot of people take the term free verse literally, with the result that there is more bad free verse written today than one can easily shake a stick at. Most of it hopes to recommend itself by deploying vaguely surrealistic images in unmetered colloquial idiom to urge acceptable opinions: that sex is a fine thing, that accurate perception is better than dull, that youth is probably a nicer condition than age, that there is more to things than their appearances…that corporations are corrupt…and that women get a dirty deal. All true and welcome. Yet what is lamentably missing is the art that makes poems re-readable once we have fathomed what they say.

Indeed, free verse without subtle dynamics has become the received, standard contemporary style, as John Hollander notices: "At the present time in the United States, there is a widespread, received free-verse style marked by a narrow (25-30 em) format, strong use of line-ending as a syntactical marker, etc., which plays about the same role in the ascent to paradise as the received Longfellow style did a century ago." Or, we can add, as the received mechanical heroic-couplet style two centuries ago.

— Paul Fussell, from *Poetic Meter and Poetic Form*

A major objection to free verse as it has been written by H. D., Dr. Williams, and perhaps others: [Free verse] tends to a rapid run-over line, so that the poem, or in the case of a fairly long poem, the stanza or paragraph, is likely to be the most important rhythmic unit, the lines being secondary…The result is a kind of breathless rush, which may very well be exciting, but which tends to exclude or to falsify all save a certain kind of feeling, by enforcing what I have called...a convention of heightened intensity.

—Yvor Winters, from *In Defense of Reason*

In free verse the only norm, so far as the structure of the foot is concerned, is perpetual variation, and the only principle governing the selection of any foot is a feeling of rhythmical continuity...[which] inevitably results in the species of inflexibility which we have seen equally in the fast meters of Williams and in the slow meters of Pound. The free-verse poet, however, achieves effects roughly comparable to those of substitution in the old meters in two ways: first by the use of lines of irregular length, a device which he employs more commonly than does the poet of the old meters and with an effect quite foreign to the effect of too few or of extra feet in the old meters; and, secondly, since the norm is perpetual variation, by the approximate repetition of a foot or of a series of feet. It is a question whether such effects can be employed with a subtlety equal to that of fine substitution.

—Yvor Winters, from *In Defense of Reason*

What are our metrical languages? Of the untraditional there is that heterogeneity of procedures, often on no discernible principles, that we call free verse, from the scriptural line of Whitman to the letters falling down the page in organic form as they spell "rain." Much of this is based on writing, on print. The lineation is determined by stipulation and whimsy, the placing on the page, with no phonetic principle unless in reading and reciting it one gives a phonetic signal at the arbitrary line-ends. But such signals, unless they coincide with idiomatic ones, are affected pronunciation.

Early free verse, however, and much still written, has a discernible principle. I call it grammatical meter: a line may end at any terminal juncture, any completed grammatical unit. If the line is short, as in much Imagistic verse, the sentence is, in effect, diagrammed; one might call it parsing meter. Some charming things were done with it; for example, Stevens' Disillusionment of Ten O'Clock...[Another type:] parasitic meter. The term is descriptive and pejorative. Such meter presupposes a meter by law which it uses, alludes to, traduces, returns to. To perceive it one must have firmly in mind the prior tradition from which it departs and to which it returns. The locus classicus is Eliot's "the most interesting verse which has yet been written in our language has been done by taking a very simple form, like the iambic pentameter, and constantly withdrawing from it, or taking no form at all, and constantly approximating to a very simple one. It is this contrast between fixity and flux, this unperceived evasion of monotony, which is the very life of verse." ...it was Eliot, perhaps, who most exploited parasitic meter.

— J. V. Cunningham, from *Tradition and Poetic Structure*

If by prosodies we mean systems or forms of versification evolved in Europe during this millennium and used by her finest poets, we can distinguish two main species, the syllabic system and the metrical one and a subspecific form belonging to the second species (but not inconsistent with certain syllabic compositions), cadential poetry, in which all that matters is lilt depending on random numbers of accents placed at random intervals. A fourth form, which is specifically vague and is rather a catchall than a definite category (not yet having been instrumental in producing great poetry), takes care of unrhymed free verse, which, except for the presence of typographical turnpikes, grades insensibly into prose, from a taxonomic point of view.

—Vladimir Nabokov, from "Notes on Prosody"

For when the single line is the unit of composition it must contain some minute torsion, something to justify its separate existence.

— Hugh Kenner, from *The Pound Era*

...the second doggerel of broken-down blank verse.

— George Saintsbury, from *A History of English Prosody*

A phrase or part of a phrase or a succession of phrases is given a special rhythmic unity—or its rhythmic form made salient—by being set apart as a line. The line invites us to find in the succession of words a rhythmical unity beyond what they have in a passage of prose; or, in a very short line, to experience more saliently the speech rhythm of the word or phrase. At least this is what much free verse evidently intends.

The rhythmically compelling phrase is effective in prose or metre or free verse.

To complain that free verse is just prose chopped up into lines ignores the fact that all the prose we ever read is chopped up into lines; we rightly pay no attention to them. But the line of free verse demands attention, not as a typographical whim but as the outline of a rhythmical unit which interacts with other language patterns.

– D. W. Harding, from *Words Into Rhythm*

It is all too easy to take a piece of non-metrical language and find rhythmic ingenuities in it; the characteristic mixture of repetition and variety in the movement of English produces flows and eddies, echoes and inversions, that would look like the work of a skilful designer if they were not ubiquitous. Much discussion of the rhythms of literary prose or free verse falls into this trap, and it is difficult to know how to avoid it when the only certain rhythmic effects are the obvious and therefore uninteresting ones.

A sense of rhythmic regularity in English, of stresses functioning as beats, is created when the number of unstressed syllables between stresses is for the most part limited to one or two, and further heightened when the beats fall into groups corresponding to common underlying rhythms; this establishes in the reader's mind a metrical set, which simplifies the stress contrasts of the language and makes possible certain limited syllabic variations. But there is a border area, where regularity remains only half-realized, and a shadowy metrical set prevents sense and syntax from wholly determining the rhythmic character of the line, but does not in itself govern the movement of the verse. Many "free verse" poets operate in this territory.

— Derek Attridge, from *The Rhythms of English Poetry*

[Free Verse:] Many variants can be found under this general heading. The extreme case occurs when prose is simply cut into lines, which may or may not be end-stopped. What this does is to summon forth our verse-reading habits, encourage us to pay more attention to the cadences and the phonetic texture. The rhythm of the prose is perhaps slightly heightened in the way, and it may even be altered a little, if the lines as set out do not coincide exactly with the phrasing but include some enjambment. Frequently, however, free verse moves some distance nearer to regularity and pattern. The lines may be grouped in twos or threes or other sets with a good deal of parallel or balance and contrast. Lines may be kept to approximately the same length— they may even tend to be organized with two, or three, or four major stresses, so that the effect is of somewhat irregular accentual verse. As free verse moves towards pattern it moves from being vers libre to vers libere.

— James McAuley, from *Versification*

The thing is that "free verse" since Whitman's time has led us astray...Whitman, great as he was in his instinctive drive, was also the cause of our going astray. I among the rest have much to answer for. No verse can be free, it must be governed by some measure, but not by the old measure. There Whitman was right but there, at the same time, his leadership failed him. The time was not ready for it. We have to return to some measure but a measure consonant with our time and not a mode so rotten than it stinks.

We have no measure by which to guide ourselves except a purely instinctive one which we feel but do not name. I am not speaking of verse which has long since been frozen into a rigid mold signifying its death, but of verse which shows that it has been touched with some dissatisfaction with its present state.

It is all over the page at the mere whim of the man who has composed it. This will not do. Certainly an art which implies a discipline as the poem does, a rule, a measure, will not tolerate it. There is no measure to guide us, no recognizable measure.

Relativity gives us the cue… We have today to do with the poetic, as always, but a relatively stable foot, not a rigid one. That is all the difference…We live in a new world, pregnant with tremendous possibility for enlightenment but sometimes, being old, I despair of it…

Without measure we are lost. But we have lost even the ability to count. Actually we are not as bad as that. Instinctively we have continued to count as always but it has become not a conscious process and being unconscious has descended to a low level of the invention. There are a few exceptions but there is no one among us who is consciously aware of what he is doing. I have accordingly made a few experiments.

        — W. C. Williams, from *The Williams Carlos Williams Reader*

A manifestation of form sense is the sense the poet's ear has of some rhythmic norm peculiar to a particular poem, from which the individual lines depart and to which they return. I heard Henry Cowell [American composer] tell that the drone in Indian music is known as the horizon note. Alkresch, the painter, sent me a quotation from Emerson: "The health of the eye demands a horizon." This sense of the beat or pulse underlying the whole I think of as the horizon note of the poem. It interacts with the nuances or forces of feeling which determine emphasis on one word or another, and decides to a great extent what belongs to a given line. It relates the needs of that feeling-force which dominates the cadence to the needs of the surrounding parts and so to the whole.

        — Denise Everton, from *New and Selected Essays*

Really the organization of poetry has moved to a further articulation in which the rhythmic and sound structure now becomes not only evident but a primary coherence in the total organization of what's being experienced. In conversation, you see, this is not necessarily the case. It largely isn't, although people speaking (at least in American speech) do exhibit clusters of this isochronous pattern of phrase groups with one primary stress; so there is a continuing rhythmic insistence in conversation. But this possibility has been increased in poetry so that now the rhythmic and sound organization have been given a very marked emphasis in the whole content. Prose rhythms in poetry are simply one further possibility of articulating pace; these so-called prose rhythms tend to be slower so that therefore they give perhaps a useful drag.

I tend to pause slightly after each line. These terminal endings give me a way of both syncopating and indicating a rhythmic measure. I think of those lines as something akin to the bar in music—they state the rhythmic modality. They indicate the basic rhythm of the poem.

– Robert Creeley, from *The Collected Prose of Robert Creeley*

EXAMPLES & COMMENT

Dark eyes,
O woman of my dreams,
Ivory sandaled,
There is none like thee among the dancers,
None with swift feet.

I have not found thee in the tents,
In the broken darkeness.
I have not found thee at the well-head
Among the women with pitchers.

Thine arms are as a young sapling under the bark;
Thy face as a river with lights...

        — Ezra Pound, from "Dance Figure"

O mother
what have I left out
O mother
what have I forgotten
O mother
farewell
with a long black shoe
farewell
with Communist Party and a broken stocking
farewell
with six dark hairs on the wen of your breast
farewell
with your old dress and a long black beard around the vagina
farewell
with your sagging belly
with your fear of Hitler
with your mouth of bad short stories
with your fingers of rotten mandolins
with your arms of fat Paterson porches
with your belly of strikes and smokestacks

with your chin of Trotsky and the Spanish War
with your voice singing for the decaying overbroken workers
with your nose of bad lay with your nose of the smell of the pickles of Newark. . .

— Allen Ginsberg, from "Kaddish"

I have never been one to write by rule, even by my own rules. Let's begin with the rule of counted syllables, in which all poems have been written hitherto. That has become tiresome to my ear.

Finally, the stated syllables, as is the best of present-day free verse, have become entirely divorced from the beat, that is the measure. The musical pace proceeds without them.

Therefore the measure, that is to say, the count, having got rid of the words, which held it down, is returned to the *music*.

The words, having been freed, have been allowed to run all over the map, "free," as we have mistakenly thought. This has amounted to no more (in Whitman and others) than no discipline at all.

But if we keep in mind the *tune* which the lines (not necessarily the words) make in our ears, we are ready to proceed.

By measure I mean musical pace. Now, with music in our ears the words need only be taught to keep as distinguished an order, as chosen a character, as regular, according to the music, as in the best of prose.

By its *music* shall the best of modern verse be known and the *resources* of the music. The refinement of the poem, its subtlety, is not to be known by the elevation of the words but—the words don't so much matter—by the resources of the *music*.

To give you an example from my own work—not that I know anything about what I myself have written:

(count) —not that I ever count when writing but, at best, the lines must be capable of being counted, that is to say, measured— (believe it or not).—At that I may, half consciously, even count the measure under my breath as I write.—

(approximate example)

    1) The smell of the heat is boxwood
        2) when rousing us
            3) a movement of the air
   4) stirs ours thoughts
      5) that had no life in them
         6) to a life, a life in which

(or)

   1) Mother of God! Our Lady!
      2) the heart
         3) is an unruly master
   4) Forgive us our sins
     5) as we
        6) forgive
   7) those who have sinned against

Count a single beat to each numeral. You may not agree with my ear, but that is the way I count the line. Over the whole poem it gives a pattern to the meter that can be felt as a new measure.

                       — W.C. Williams, in a letter to Richard Eberhart, 1954

The foot which I have used consists of one heavily accented syllable, an unlimited number of unaccented syllables, and an unlimited number of syllables of secondary accent.

The secondary accent is discernible as type if the poet makes it so. A dozen types of accent are possible in theory, but in practice no more than two can be kept distinct in the mind; in fact it is not always easy to keep two.

Ambiguity of accent will be more common in such verse as I am describing than in the older verse, but up to a certain point this is not a defect, this kind of ambiguity being one of the chief beauties of Milton's verse, for example.

Quantity will obviously complicate this type of foot more than it will the foot of more familiar meters.

The free verse foot is very long, or is likely to be.

Two of the principles of variation—substitution and immeasurably variable degrees of accent—which are open to the poet employing the old meters, are not open to the poet employing free verse, for, as regards substitution, there is no foot to indicate which syllables are to be considered accented, but the accented syllable must identify itself in relation to the entire line, the result being that accents are of fairly fixed degrees, and certain ranges of possible accent are necessarily represented by gaps. In free verse, the only norm, so far as the structure of the foot is concerned, is perpetual variation, and the only principle governing the selection of any foot is a feeling of rhythmical continuity; and on the other hand the norm of the line, a certain number of accents of recognizably constant intensity, and in spite of the presence of the relatively variable secondary accents, inevitably results in the species of inflexibility which we have seen equally in the fast meters of Williams and in the slow meters of Pound.

—Yvor Winters, from *In Defense of Reason*

Old age is
a flight of small
cheeping birds
skimming
bare trees
above a snow glaze.
Gaining and failing,
they are buffeted
by a dark wind...

—W.C. Williams, scanned by Winters

135

Or there may be an uneven mixture of regularity and of irregularity, which is the possibility least to be desired.

The opening of Richard Aldington's *Choricos* illustrates the mixture of free and regular verse.

The ancient songs
Pass deathward mournfully.

Cold lips that sing no more, and withered wreaths,
Regretful eyes, and drooping breasts and wings—
Symbols of ancient songs
Mournfully passing
Down to the great white surges ...

The first four lines comprise three perfect lines of blank verse.

—Yvor Winters (c. 1930), from *Primitivism and Decadence*

There were no undesirables or girls on my set,
when I was a boy at Mattapoisett—
only Mother, still her Father's daughter.
Her voice was still electric
with a hysterical, unmarried panic,
when she read to me from the Napoleon book ... .
and I, bristling and manic,
skulked in the attic,
and got two hundred French generals by name,
from A to V—from Augereau to Vandamme.
I used to dope myself asleep,
naming those unprounceables like sheep.

LOWELL: Then there are others where I wrote specifically at the time in regular meter and just felt they didn't work at all and ripped them up, like the Commander Lowell one. It was once a couplet poem and ... it was perfectly regular. I just knocked it out but a lot of the couplets remain as rhymes.... The free-verse poems—I think that the whole trick is that you've got to say to yourself, this isn't going to be scanned while you write it, that you're not given any rules. Then you may toss in little rhymes, or toss in lines where the beat is quite marked and an iambic line comes through.... . It just doesn't have any rules; it has that freedom.

R. P. WARREN: Cal, may I ask if you have any principle about our line lengths. Do you hear your line. . . and God tells you? Is that it?

LOWELL: I think it's partly visual, sometimes I like to see a poem go down the page in short lines, and when there's a long, looping line, I'm very conscious of that and I couldn't say why it's good, or if it's good, I mean, and but part of it's visual and you wonder in a free-verse poem, if you read it aloud to someone, if that person could ever—copy down every word—could ever get your line pattern. And a very funny thing happened. I wrote out a Williams' poem about parking lots and it's read like a very clouded, rhetorical Faulkner paragraph. But when you read it in quatrains of lines all equal length in Williams, it looked very light and springy. I don't know. It doesn't disturb me that someone couldn't get your line scheme from just knowing the words.

— Robert Lowell, from "Commander Lowell"

The dislocation of syntax generates a prosody of sorts in Amy Lowell's "Violin Sonata by Vincent D'Indy":

A little brown room in a sea of fields,
Fields pink as rose-mallows
Under a fading rose-mallow sky.

Four candles on a tall iron candlestick.
Clustered like altar lights.
Above, the models four brown Chinese junks
Sailing round the brown walls,
Silent and motionless.

Again we have free-floating images without grammatical orientation. By carefully suppressing all verbs, Amy Lowell presents rather than comments on an experience. Such method denies the importance of human action in poetry and limits it to perceptual reporting. As part of the reform movement in modern poetry, Imagist techniques were historically useful in clearing out excessive sentiment and cleaning up the rhetoric; keeping an eye, unclouded by the steam of one's own emotions, on the object was the salutary aim of Imagism. But...

—Harvey Gross, from *Sound and Form in Modern Poetry*

The river's tent is broken; the last fingers of leaf
Clutch and sink into the wet bank. The wind
Crosses the brown land, unheard. The nymphs are departed.
Sweet Thames, run softly, till I end my song.
The river bears no empty bottles, sandwich papers,
Silk handkerchiefs, cardboard boxes, cigarette ends
Or other testimony of summer nights. The nymphs are departed.
And their friends, the loitering heirs of city directors;
Departed, have left no addresses.
By the waters of Leman I sat down and wept...
Sweet Thames, run softly till I end my song,
Sweet Thames, run softly, for I speak not loud or long.

—T.S. Eliot, from *The Waste Land*, III

In this example, even the lines which are not quotations from or variants of lines of earlier verse show a distinct preference for single nonstresses between stresses, spiced with a fair number of double nonstresses a few instances of three nonstresses or none. There is only one sequence of four nonstresses ("testimony of"), and none with more. The result is a rhythm distinctly different from that of prose, heightened by a division into lines that correspond roughly to the favoured lengths of regular English verse (all but one have between nine and fourteen syllables), by the quotations from metrical poetry, and diction and content. If any metrical set were to emerge it would be for five-beat lines, but since the five-beat grouping demands strict adherence to the normal deviation rules, the variations here are sufficient to keep regularity just out of reach. As a result, the lines establish associations with the tradition of English verse, but in an oblique and ironic way, neither committing the poem to that tradition, nor wholly challenging it.

— Derek Attridge, from *The Rhythms of English Poetry*

LONG-LINE FREE VERSE, TYPE A: THE DITHYRAMBIC OR ORACULAR: WHITMAN, THE BIBLE, ETC.

The heavens declare the glory of God; and the firmament showeth his
  handywork.
Day unto day uttereth speech, and night sheweth knowledge.
There is no speck or language, where their voice is not heard...
His going forth is from the end of heaven, and his circuit unto the ends
of it: and there is nothing hid from the heat thereof.
The law of the Lord is perfect, converting the soul: the testimony of
the Lord is sure, making wise the simple
The statutues of the lord are right, rejoicing the heart: the
commandment of the Lord is pure, enlightening the eyes...
More to be desired are they than god, yea, than much fine gold:
sweeter also than the honey and the honeycomb...
Let the word of my mouth, and the meditation of my heart, be
acceptable in thy sight, O Lord, my strength, and my redeemer.

—Psalm 19, from King James Bible

Give unto the Lord, O ye mighty, give unto the Lord glory and strength.
Give unto the Lord the glory due unto his name; worship the Lord in
  the beauty of holiness.
The voice of the Lord is upon the waters: the God of glory
  thundereth: the Lord is upon many waters.
The voice of the Lord is powerful; the voice of the Lord is full of majesty.
The voice of the Lord breaketh the cedars; yea, the Lord breaketh the
  cedars of Lebanon.

He maketh them also to skip like a calf; Lebanon and Sirion like a
young unicorn.
The voice of the Lord divideth the flames of fire...

— Psalm 29, from King James Bible

Let Elizure rejoice with the Partridge, who is a prisoner of state
and is proud of his keepers.
For I am not without authority in my jeopardy, which I derive
inevitably from the glory of the name of the Lord.
Let Shedeur rejoice with Pyrausta, who dwelleth in a medium
of fire, which God hath adapted for him.
For I bless God whose name is Jealous—and there is a zeal to
deliver us from everlasting burnings.
Let Shelumiel rejoice with Olor, who is of a goodly savour, and
the very look of him harmonizes the mind.
For my estimation is good even amongst the slanderers and my
memory shall rise for a sweet savour unto the Lord...

— Christopher Smart, from "Jubilate Agno"

As flies the unconstant sun, over Larmon's grassy hill, so pass the
tales of old along my soul by night! When bards are removed to
their place, when harps are hung in Selma's hall, then comes a
voice to Ossian, and awakes his soul! It is the voice of years that
are gone! They roll before me with all their deeds! I seize the
tales as they pass, and pour them forth in song. Nor a troubled
stream is the song of the King, it is like the rising of music from
Lutha of the strings. Lutha of many strings, not silent are thy
streamy rocks, when the white hands malvina move upon the
harp! Light of the shadowy thoughts, that fly across my soul,
daughter of Toscar of helmets, wilt thou not hear the song? We
call back, maid of Lutha the years that have rolled away!

— James MacPherson, from *Oian-Morul: a Poem*

I am made to sow the thistle for wheat; the nettle for a nourishing dainty.
I have planted a false oath in the earth; it has brought forth a poison tree.
I have chosen the serpent for a councellor and the dog
For a schoolmaster to my children.

I have blotted out from light and living the dove and nightingale,
And I have caused the earth worm to beg from door to door.
I have taught the thief a secret path into the house of the just,
I have taught pale artifice to spread his nets upon the morning.
My heavens are brass, my earth is iron, my moon a clod of clay,
My sun a pestilence burning at noon and a vapour of death in night.

        —William Blake, from *The Four Zoas*

To bathe in the Waters of Life; to wash off the Not Human,
I come in Self-annihilation and the grandeur of Inspiration,
To cast off Rational Demonstration by Fait in the Saviour,
To cast off the rotten rags of Memory by Inspiration,
To cast off Bacon, Locke and Newton from Albion's covering,
To take off his filty garments, and clothe him with Imagination,
To cast aside from Poetry all that is not Inspiration,
That it no longer shall dare to mock with the aspersion of madness
Cast on the Inspired, by the tame high finisher of paltry Blots
Indefinite, or paltry Rhymes, or paltry Harmonies.

        — Blake, from *Milton*

Out of the cradle endlessly rocking,
Out of the mocking-bird's throat, the musical shuttle,
Out of the Ninth-month midnight,
Over the sterile sands and the fields beyond, where the child leaving
his bed wander'd alone bareheaded, barefoot,
Down from the shower'd halo,
Up from the mystic play of shadows twining and twisting as if they
 were alive,
Out from the patches of briers and blackberries,
From the memories of the bird that chanted to me,
From your memories, sad brother, from the fitful rising and fallings I heard,
From under that yellow half-moon late-risen and swollen as if with tears...

  —Walt Whitman, from "Out of the Cradle Endlessly Rocking"

The early lilacs became part of this child,
And grass and white and red morning-glories, and white and red clover,
And the song of the phoebe-bird

And the Third-month lambs and the sow's pink-faint litter, and the
    mare's foal and the cow's calf,
And the noisy brood of the barnyard or by the mire of the pond-side,
And fish suspending themselves so curiously below there, and the
    beautiful curious liquid,
And the water-plants with their graceful flat beads, all became part of him.
The field-sprouts of Fourth-month and Fifth-month became part of him...

        –Whitman, from "There Was A Child Went Forth"

One's self I sing, a simple separate person,
Yet utter the word democratic, the word En-Masse.

Of physiology from top to toe I sing,
Not physiognomy alone nor brain alone is worthy for the Muse,
I say the from complete is worthier far,
The Female equally with the Male I sing...

        –Whitman, from "One's-Self I Sing"

Je chante le soi-meme, une simple personne separee,
Pourtant tout le mot democratique, le mot En Masse.
C'est de la physiologies du haut en bas, que je chante,
La physionomie seule, le cerveau seul, ce n'est pas digne de la
Muse; je dis que L'Etre complet en est bien plus digé
C'est le feminine a l'egal du male, que je chante...

        – Laforgue, from "Je Chante le Soi-Meme"

  A child said what is the grass? Fetching it to me with full hands;
  How could I answer the child? I do not know what it is any
    more than he.

The passage above when scanned be periods (periodicity? Equal
time-lapses between stresses?) reveal a highly developed meter.
Each line of a couplet of seven-stress verse is broken by a medial
caesura at precisely the same point, after the third stress. The
rhythmic equivalence between the two lines is striking, and it

is not caused by either logical recurrence or the iteration of identical phrases. This purely rhythmic patterning is quite as characteristic of Whitman's writing as the logical balance.

– Sculley Bradley, from *The American Tradition in Literature*

The rhyme and uniformity of perfect poems show the free growth of metrical laws and bud from them as unerringly and loosely as lilacs or roses on a bush, and take shapes as compact as the shapes of chestnuts and oranges and melons and pears, and shed the perfume impalpable to form.

– Whitman (1855), from the preface to *Leaves of Grass*

Of his own poetry: "a perpetual series of what might be called *ejaculations*."

– Whitman

In more than 10,500 lines of verse in *Leaves of Grass* there are only 20 run-on lines.

Bavarian gentians, big and dark, only dark
Darkening the day-time torch-like with the smoking blueness of Pluto's gloom,
Ribbed and torch-like with their blaze of darkness spread blue
Down flattening into points, flattened under the sweep of white day
Torch-flower of the blue-smoking darkness, Pluto's dark-blue daze,
Black lamps from the halls of Dis, burning dark blue,
Giving off darkness, blue darkness, as Demeter's pale lamps give off light,
Lead me then, lead me the way.

– D.H. Lawrence, from "Bavarian Gentians"

who walked all night with their shoes full of blood on the snowbank
    docks waiting for a door in the East River to open to a room full of
    steamboat and opium,
who created great suicidal dramas on the apartment cliff-banks of
    the Hudson under the wartime blue floodlight of the moon and
    their heads shall be crowned with laurel in oblivion,
who ate the lamb stew of the imagination or digested the crab at the

muddy bottom of the rivers of the Bowery,
who wept at the romance of the streets with their pushcarts full of
  onions and bad music,
who sat in boxes breathing in the darkness under the bridge, and rose
  up to build harpsichords in their lofts,
who coughed on the sixth floor of Harlem crowned with flame under
  the tubercular sky surrounded by orange crates of theology,
who scribble all night rocking and rolling over lofty incantations
which in the yellow morning were stanzas of gibberish...

> — Allen Ginsberg (1956), from "Howl"

I misunderstand Greek entirely;
I find ancient Greece very hard to understand: I probably
  misunderstand it;
I misunderstand spoken German about 98% of the time, like the
  cathedral in the middle of a town;
I misunderstand "Beautiful Adventure"; I also think I probably
  misunderstand La Nausea by Jean-Paul Sartre...
I probably misunderstand misunderstanding itself—I misunderstand
  the Via margutta in Rome, or via della Vite, no matter what street,
  all of them...

> — Kenneth Koch, from "Taking a Walk With You"

Me clairvoyant,
Me conscious of you, old camarado,
Needing no telescope, lorgnette, field-glass, opera-glass, myopic pince-nez,
Me piercing two thousand years with eye naked and not ashamed;
The crown cannot hide you from me;
Musty old feudal-heraldic trappings cannot hide you from me,
I perceive that you drink.
(I am drinking with you. I am as drunk as you are.)
I see you are inhaling tobacco, puffing, smoking, spitting
(I do not object to your spitting.)
You prophetic of American largeness,
You anticipating the broad masculine manners of these States;
I see in you also there are movements, tremors, tears, desire for the melodious,
I salute your three violinists, endlessly making vibrations,
Rigid, relentless, capable of going on for ever;

They play my accompaniment; but I shall take no notice of any
   accompaniment;
I myself am a complete orchestra.
So long.

                    — G.K. Chesterton, from "Variations of an Air"

Les negociateurs de Tyr et crux-la qui vent a leers affaires
   aujourd'hui sur l'eau dans de grandes imaginations mecaniques,
Ceux que le mouchoir par les ailes de cette mouette encore
   Accompagne quad le bras qui l'agitait a disparu,
Ceux a qui leur vigne et leur champ ne suffisaient pas, mais
   Monsieur await son idée personelle sur l'Amerique,
Ceux qui sont parties por toujours et qui n'arriveront pas non plus,
Tous ces devoreurs de la distance, c'est le mar elle-meme
   A present qu'on leer sert, penses-tu qu'ils en auront assez?

                    — Paul Claudel, from "Ballade"

Yes queue este fue uno de los enterrados con el reloj de plata
   en el solsillo bajo del chaleco,
para queue a la una en punto desaparecieran las islas
para que a las dos en punto a los toros mas negros se les volviera
   Blanca la cabeza,
para que a last res en punto una bala de plomo perforara la
   hostia solitaria expuesta en la custodia de una iglesia perdida en el
   cruce de dos veredas: una camino de un prostibulo y otra de un
   balneario de aguas minerals (y el reloj sobre el muerto)...

          — Rafael Alberta; the poet called long lines
            of this type "painting on a wall."

When you traveled the white wake of our going sent your shadow
   below, but when you arrived it was there to greet you. You had your
   shadow.
The doorways you entered lifted your shadow from you and when you
   went out, gave it back. You had your shadow.
Even when you forgot your shadow, you found it again; it had been
   with you.

Once in the country the shade of a tree covered your shadow and you
were not known.
Once in the country you thought your shadow had been cast by
somebody else. You said nothing.
Your clothes carried your shadow inside; when you took them off, it
spread like the dark of your past.
And your words that float like leaves in an air that is lost, in a place no
one knows, gave you back your shadow.
Your friends gave you back your shadow.
Your enemies gave you back your shadow. They said it was heavy and
would cover your grave...

— Mark Strand, from "Elegy for My Father"

LONG-LINE FREE VERSE, TYPE B: THE
LOOSENED BLANK-VERSE LINE

A selective chronology of Stevens passages in which the blank-verse line
is progressively loosened:

There is not any haunt of prophecy,
Nor any old chimera of the grave,
Neither the golden underground, nor isle
Melodious, where spirits gat them home,
Nor visionary south, nor cloudy palm
Remote on heaven's hill, that has endured
Like her remembrance of awakened birds,
Or her desire for June and evening, tipped
By the consummation of the swallow's wings.

(1915, from "Sunday Morning")

On a blue island in a sky-wide water

The wild orange trees continued to bloom and to bear
Long after the planter's death. A few limes remained,

Where his house had fallen, three scraggy trees weighted
With garbled green. These were the planter's turquoise
And his orange blotches, these were his zero green,

A green baked greener in the greenest sun.

(1942, from "It Must Change")

The trees had been mended, as an essential exercise
In an inhuman meditation, larger than her own.
The winds like dogs watched over her at night.

She wanted nothing he could not bring her by coming alone.
She wanted no fetching. His arms would be her necklace
And her belt, the final fortune of their desire.

But was it Ulysses? Or was it only the warmth of the sun
On her pillow? The thought kept beating in her like a heart.
The two kept beating together. It was only day.

(1952, from "The World as Meditation")

Examples of Eliot's "Websterean" verse:

I that am of your blood was taken from you
For your better health; look no more upon's,
But cast it to the ground regardlessly,
Let the common sewer take it from distinction...

(1927, from the essay "Thomas Middleton")

I that was near your heart was removed therefrom
To lose beauty in terror, terror in inquisition...

(1920, from "Gerontion")

To explore the womb, or tomb, or dreams; all these are usual
Pastimes and drugs, and features of the press:

And always will be, some of them especially
When there is distress of nations and perplexity
Whether on the shores of Asia, or in the Edgar Road...

(1941, from Four Quartets)

The mauve and greenish souls of the little Millwins
were seen lying along the upper seats.

— Pound (1913), from "Lustra"

While my hair was still cut straight across my forehead
Played I about the front gate, pulling flowers.
You came by on bamboo stilts, playing horse,
You walked about my seat, playing with blue plums.
And we went on living in the village of Chokan:
Two small people, without dislike or suspicion.

— Pound (1915), from "A River Merchant's Wife: A Letter" after Li Po

...It is now she begins to sing—at first quite low
Then loud, and at last with a jazzy madness—
The song of her whistle screaming at curves,
Of deafening tunnels, brakes, innumerable bolts.
And always light, aerial, underneath
Goes the elate meter of her wheels.

— Stephen Spender (1933), from "The Express"

Tired and unhappy, you think of houses
Soft-carpeted and warm in the December evening,
While snow's white pieces fall past the window.

— Delmore Schwartz (1938), from "Tired and
Unhappy, You Think of Houses"

That speaks, in the Wild of things, delighting riddles
To the soul that listens, trusting...
                                        Poor senseless life.

                    — Randall Jarrell, from "A Girl in a Library"

Always the silence, the gesture, the specks of birds
suspended on invisible threads above the site,
o the smoke rising solemnly, pulled by threads.

                    — Elizabeth Bishop, from "Over 2000 Illustrations
                              and a Complete Concordance"

The night is warm and clean and without wind.
The stone-white moon waits above the rooftops
and above the nearby river. Every street is still.

                    — Mark Strand, from "Leopardi"

Et tu bois cet alcohol brilliant comme ta vie
Ta vie que tu bois comme une eau-de-vie

Tu marches vers Auteuil tu veux aller chez toi a pied
Dormir parmi tes fetiches d'Oceanie et de Guinee
Ils sont des Christ d'une autre forme et d'une autre croyance
Ce sont les Christ inferieurs des obscures experances

                    — Apollinaire (1912), from "Zone:"Vers libere; that
                              is, loosened alexandrines in this case.)

LONG-LINE FREE VERSE, TYPE C: PROSE
BROKEN UP INTO LINES

It is 12:20 in New York a Friday
three days after Bastille day, yes
it is 1959 and I go get a shoeshine

because I will get off the 4:19 in Easthampton
at 7:15 and then go straight to dinner
and I don't know the people who will feed me

> — Frank O'Hara, from "The Day Lady Died"

It's 8:54 a.m. in Brooklyn it's the 28th of July and
it's probably 8:54 in Manhattan but I'm
in Brooklyn I'm eating English muffins and drinking
pepsi and I'm thinking of how Brooklyn is New
York City too how odd I usually think of it as
Something all its own like Bellows Falls like Little
Chute like Uijonjbu

> —Ted Berrigan, from "Sonnet XXXVI" after Frank O'Hara

I was a girl waiting by the roadside for boyfriend to come
in his car. I was pregnant, I should have been going to high
school. I walked up the road when he didn't come, over a bridge;
I saw a sleeping man. I came to the Elwha River—grade
school classes—I went and sat down with the children.

> — Gary Snyder, from "The Elwha River"
> possibly intended to be read as prose

SHORT-LINE FREE VERSE, TYPE A: THE "IMAGIST" LINE

I saw the first pear
as it fell—
the honey-seeking, golden-banded,
the yellow swarm
was not more fleet than I,
(spare us from loveliness)
and I fell prostrate,
crying:
you have flayed us

with your blossoms,
spare us the beauty
of fruit-trees...

— H.D., from "Orchard"

The houses are haunted
By white night-gowns.
None are green,
Or purple with green rings,
Or green with yellow rings,
Or yellow with blue rings.
None are strange,
With socks of lace
And beaded ceintures.
People are not going
To dream of baboons and periwinkles.
Only, here and there, an old sailor,
Drunk and asleep in his boots,
Catches tigers
In red weather.

— Wallace Stevens, "Disillusionment of Ten O'clock"

The night is of the color
Of a woman's arms
Night, the female,
Obscure,
Fragrant and supple,
Conceals herself.
A pool shines,
Like a bracelet,
Shaken in a dance.

— Stevens, from "Six Significant Landscapes"

In Oklahoma,
Bonnie and Josie,
Dressed in calico,
Danced around a stump.

They cried,
"Ohoyaho,
Ohoo"...
Celebrating the marriage
Of flesh and air.

— Stevens, from "Life is Motion"

Virgin of boorish births,

Swiftly in the nights,
In the porches of Key West,
Behind the bougainvilleas,
After the guitar is asleep,
Lasciviously as the wind,
You come tormenting,
Insatiable,

When you might sit,
A scholar of darkness,
Sequestered over the sea,
Wearing a clear tiara
Of red and blue and red,
Sparkling, solitary, still,
In the high sea-shadow...

— Stevens, from "O Florida, Venereal Soil"

Bah! I have sung women in three cities,
But it is all the same;
And I will sing of the sun.

Lips, words, and you snare them,
Dreams, words, and they are as jewels,
Strange spells of old deity,
Ravens, nights, allurement:
And they are not;
Having become the souls of song.

Eyes, dreams, lips, and the night goes.
Being upon the road once more,
They are not…

— Pound, from "Cino"

O helpless few in my country!
O remnant enslaved!

Artists broken against her,
Astray, lost in the villages,
Mistrusted, spoken against,

Lovers of beauty, starved,
Thwarted with systems,
Helpless against the control…

Take thought:
I have weathered the storm,
I have beaten out my exile.

— Pound, from "The Rest"

At night,
The lake is a wide silence,
Without imagination.

—Walter Conrad Arensberg from "Voyage à L'Afini"

The ice is glazing over,
Torn lanterns flutter,
On the leaves is snow.

— John Gould Fletcher, from "The Blue Symphony"

The white body of the evening
Is torn into scarlet,
Slashed and gouged and seared

Into crimson,
And hung ironically
With garlands of mist.

And the wind
Blowing over London from Flanders
Has a bitter taste.

— Richard Aldington, from "Sunsets"

Clear eyed flame
betrayer of earth
draw back from the sun!
Go in once more
to the wet grains, your secret.

— Conrad Aiken, from "Illusions"

Fourteen queens:
Seven in gold,
Five in green,
And two
Are covered each
With an old-rose
Silk sari
Dotted with vermilion discs
And fringed with dusky gold.

— Ferdinand Reyher, from "Kaleidoscopes"

The wind in the pine trees
Is like the shuffling of waves
Upon the wooden sides of boat.

— Amy Lowell, from "The Fisherman's Wife"

Turned-over roots
With bleached veins

Twined like fine hair,
Each clump in the shape of a root.

                —Theodore Roethke, from "Flower Dump"

…bees drag their high garlands,
Heavily,
Toward hives of snow.

               — James Wright, from "In Fear of Harvests"

…A cheekbone,
A curved piece of brow,
A pale eyelid,
Float in the dark,
And now I make out
An eye, dark,
Wormed with far-off, unaccountable lights.

               — Galway Kinnell, from "Poem of Night"

And still I lie here,
bruised by rain, gored
by the tiny horns
of sprouting grass…

               — Gregory Orr, from "Song of the Invisible Corpse"

EXAMPLES FROM ROMANCE LANGUAGES:

Il peut marcher,
Il peut parler,
Il peut dormir.

Ce n'est pas facile.

Il doit porter
Ce qu'il traversa.

Et le voyage a été long
Dans les minutes.

> – Eugene Guillevic, from "L'Homme que se ferme"

Ah, Miss X, Miss X, sin sombrero,
alba sin colorette,
sola,
tan libre,
tu,
en el viento!

> – Rafael Alberta, from "A Miss X, entered en el viento el oeste"

SHORT-LINE FREE VERSE, TYPE B: SHORT LINES WITH A POSSIBLE SYLLABIC SOURCE OR ASSOCIATION

The world gains on them
detail by detail,
smell of curried sausage,
a withering in small parks –
and they are treading
between recognitions
when a light rain
tampers with the evening.

> –Thom Gunn, from "Kurfurstendamm"

so much depends
upon

a red wheel
barrow

glazed with rain
water

beside the white
chickens

— W. C. Williams, from "The Red Wheelbarrow"

You never got to recline
in the material tradition,
I never let you. Fate,

You call it, had other eyes,
for neither of us ever had
a counterpart in the way

familial traditions go...

— James Tate, from "For Mother on Father's Day"

The pure products of America
go crazy—
mountain folk from Kentucky

or the ribbed north end of
Jersey
with its isolate lakes and

valleys, its dead-mutes, thieves
old names
and promiscuity between

devil-may-care men who have taken
to railroading
out of sheer lust of adventure—

and young slatterns bathed
in filth
from Monday to Saturday

> to be tricked out that night
> with gauds
> from imaginations which have no
>
> peasant traditions to give them
> character...

— W.C. Williams, from "To Elsie"

OTHER EXAMPLES: RUNOVER OR ENJAMBED LINES

1a.
The houses are haunted
By white night-gowns.
None are green,
Or purple with green rings,
Or green with yellow rings,
Or yellow with blue rings.
None are strange
With socks of lace
And beaded ceintures.
People are not going
To dream of baboons and periwinkles.
Only, here and there, an old sailor,
Drunk and asleep in his boots,
Catches tigers
In red weather.

1b. As Williams might have done it:

or purple with green
rings, or green with
yellow rings, or
yellow with blue rings. None

Only,
here and there, an
old sailor, drunk,
and asleep in
his boots, catches
tigers in red weather.

2a.

To all the girls
of all ages
who walk up and down on

the streets of this town

2b. Lines arranged without the runovers
& so as to emphasize equivalence:

who walk up and down

on the streets of this town

silent or gabbing
putting

their feet down
one before the other
one two one two

one two they one two
pause sometimes before they pause sometimes
a store window and before a store window

reform the line and reform the line
from here from here to China
to China everywhere everywhere

back and back and forth
forth and back and forth and back and forth
and back and forth and back and forth

      —W.C. Williams (1962)
"Perpetuum Mobile" from "Some
Simple Measures in the American
    Idiom and the Variable Foot"

     3.
     Tho' I'm no Catholic
     I listen hard when the bells
     in the yellow brick-tower
     of their new church

     ring down the leaves
     ring in the frost upon them
     and the death of the flowers
     ring out the grackle

     toward the south, the sky
     darkened by them, ring in
     the new baby of Mr and Mrs
     Krantz which cannot

for the fat of its cheeks
open well its eyes, ring out
the parrot under its hood
jealous of the child

ring in Sunday morning
and old age which adds as it
takes away. Let them ring
only ring! Over the oil

painting of a young priest
on the church wall advertising
last week's Novena to St
Anthony, ring for the lame

Young man in black with
Gaunt cheeks and wearing a
Derby hat, who is hurrying
to 11 o'clock Mass (the

grapes still hanging to
the vines along the nearby
Concordia Halle like broken
teeth in the head of an

old man) Let them ring
for the eyes and ring for
the hands and ring for
the children of my friend

who no longer hears
them ring but with a smile
and in a low voice speaks
of the decisions of her

daughter and the proposals
and betrayals of her
husbands' friends. O bells
ring for the ringing!

the beginning and the end
of ringing! Ring ring
ring ring ring ring ring!
Catholic bells—!

—W.C. Williams (1935) "Catholic Bells"

HISTORICAL EXAMPLES

Variant translations of Rimbaud's "Marine":

Les chars d'argent et de cuivre—les proues d'acieret d'argent—
battent l'ecume,—soulevent les souches des ronces. Les
courants de la lande, et les ornieres immenses du reflux, filent
circulairement vers l'est, vers les piliers de la foret,—vers let
futs de la jetee, dont l'angle est heurte par des tourbillons de
lumiere.

– first published in Gustave Kahn's magazine, *La Vogue* in 1886, as prose.

Les chars d'argent et de cuivre—
Les proues d'acier et d'argent—
Battent l'ecume,—
Soulevent les souches des ronces.
Les courants de la lande,
Et les ornieres immenses du reflux,
Filent circulairement vers l'est,
Vers les pilliers de la foret,—
Vers les futs de la jetee,
Dont l'angle est heurte par des tourbillions de lumiere.

– as commonly published

Rimbaud's editor, Suzanne Bernard, comments: "Elle (cite piece) date
vraisemblablement d'une époque ou Rimbaud n'etait pas encore entierement
libere du prejuge de la versification, et se livrait, our assouplir la forme, au
meme ordre de Recherches que celui qui condor les Symbolistes au vers libre."
(1960)

Chariots of copper and of silver—
Prows of silver and of steel—
Thresh the foam,—
Upheave the stumps and brambles.
The currents of the heat,
And the enormous ruts of the ebb,
Flow circularly toward the east,

Toward the pillars of the forest,——
Toward the boles of the jetty,
Against whose edge whirlwinds of light collide.

— Louise Varese

C'est l'automne, l'automne, l'automne,
Le grand vent et toute sa sequelle
De represailles! Et de musiques!...
Rideaux tires, cloture annuelle,
Chute des feuilles, des Antigones, des Philomeles:
Mon Fossoyeur, Alas poor Yorick!
Les remue a la pelle!...

Vivent l'Amour et les feux de paille!...
Les Jeunes Filles inviolables et freles
Descendent vers la petite chapelle
Donts les chimeriques cloches
Du joli, joli demarche
Hygieniquement et elegamment les appellent.

Comme tout se fait proper autour d'elles!
Comme tout en est dimanche!

Comme on se fait dur et boudeur a leer approche!... .

— Jules Laforgue, from "Demarches"

SOME RHETORICAL FIGURES

Anaphora: the same word beginning a sequence of clauses or sentences.

Some glory in their birth, some in their skill,
Some in their wealth, some in their bodies' force,
Some in their garments—though new-fangles ill,—
Some in their hawks and hounds, some in their horse…

　　　　　　　　　　　　　－ Shakespeare, from "Sonnet 91"

I can love both fair and brown,
Her whom abundance melts, and her whom want betrays,
Her who loves loneness best, and her who masks and plays,
Her whom the country form'd, and whom the town…

　　　　　　　　　　　　　－ Donne, from "The Indifferent"

With sick and farist eyes
With doubling knees and weary bones,
　　　To thee my cries,
　　　To thee my groans,
To thee my sighs, my tears ascend…

　　　　　　　　　　　　　－ Herbert, from "Longing"

Asyndeton: words or phrases piled up without intervening conjunctions.

I came, I saw, I conquered.
Whose me seethe, he seethe sorwe al atonys,
Peyne, torment, pleynte, wo, distresses!

　　　　　　　　　　　　　－ Chaucer, from "Troilus and Criseyde"

Till then, Love, let my body reign, and let
Me travel, sojourn, snatch, plot, have, forget...

— Donne, from "Love's Usury"

And of their wonted vigor left them drain'd,
Exhausted, spiritless, afflicted, fall'n.

— Milton, from *Paradise Lost*

Here Flies of Pins extend their shining Rows,
Puffs, Powders, Patches, Bibles, Billet-doux.

— Pope, from *The Rape of the Lock*

Epistrophe: same word ending a sequence of clauses or sentences.

When I was a child, I spoke as a child, I understood as a child, I
thought as a child.

— First Corinthians

For thee explain a thing till all men doubt it,
And write about it, Goddess, and about it.

— Pope, from *The Dunciad*

Epizeuxis: same word repeated, no words intervening.

Comfort ye, comfort ye, my people.

— Isaiah 40:1

Owt of thise blake wawes for to saylle,
O wynd, o wynd, the weder gynneth clere;

— Chaucer, from "Troilus and Criseyde"

O dark, dark, dark, amid the blaze of noon.

> — Milton, from *Samson Agonistes*

Ploce: repeating the same word within a line or sequence of clauses.

And the King was much moved, and went up to the chamber over the gate, and wept; and as he went, thus he said. 'O my son Absalom, my son, my son Absalom! Would God I had died for thee, O Absalom, my son, my son!'

> — Second Samuel 18:33

When thou sigh'st thou sigh'st not wind,
But sigh'st my soul away...

> — Donne from "Song: Sweetest love, I do not go"

Yet it creates, transcending these,
Far other Worlds, and other Seas;
Annihilating all that's made
To a green Thought in a green shade.

> — Marvell, from "The Garden"

Polyptoton: repeating a word in a different form but from the same root. (Using different cases of the same word.)

And death once dead, there's no more dying then.

> — Shakespeare, from Sonnet 146

To live a life half-dead, a living death.

> — Milton, from *Samson Agonistes*

Zeugma: using the same verb to serve two or more objects.

the tank fired, and the bridge and many hopes sank.

Or stain her Honour, or her new Brocade...
Or lose her Heart, or Necklace at a Ball...
Not louder Shrieks to pitying Heav'n are cast,
When Husbands or when Lap-dogs breathe their last ...
On the rich Quilt sinks with becoming Woe,
Wrapt in a Gown, for Sickness, and for Show.

—Pope, from *The Rape of the Lock*

(The definitions and most of the examples are taken from *Classical Rhetoric in English Poetry*, by Brian Vickers.)

QUANTITATIVE VERSE IN ENGLISH

Sir Philip Sidney's rules (abridged):

1. Consonant before consonant long.
2. Single consonants commonly short, except such as have a double sound (*lack*, *will*) or such as the vowel before makes long (*hate*).
3. Vowel before vowel short, except such an exclamation as *oh!*
4. Such vowels are long as the pronunciation makes long (*glory*, *lady*), and such as seem to have a dipthong sound (*show*, *dye*).
5. Elisions, when one vowel meets with another, used indifferently as the advantage of the verse best serves (*thou art* or *th'art*). (For so it is in speech and Petrarch as well.)
6. Words derived from Latin and other languages are given English values (not for*tu*nate, though Latin is for*tu*na).
7. Some words especially short.
8. Particles used now long, now short (*but*, *or*, *to*).
9. Some words, as they have different pronunciations, to be written differently (*though* or *tho*).
10. As for *wee*, *shee*, *thee*, though spelled with a double vowel, they should be counted short, and the same with *o*, which some write double as in *doo*.

– from p. 391 of *The Poems of Sir Philip Sidney*, ed. By W.A. Ringler

METRICAL EXAMPLES

O my thoughtes' sweete foodie, my my onely owner,
   O my heavens for taste by the heavenly pleasure,
  O the fare Nymphe borne to doo woemen honor,
                          Lady my Treasure.

  Where bee now those Joyes, that I lately tasted?
    Where bee nowe those eyes ever Inly erasers?
  Where bee now those wordes never Idolly wasted,
                       Woundes to Rehersers?

  Where ys Ah that face, that a Sunne defaces?
    Where bee those welcomes by no worthe deserved?
  Where bee those movinges, the Delights, the graces?
                     Howe bee wee swerved?

      – Sir Philip Sidney, from *The Countess of Pembroke Arcadia*

Green the ways, the breath of the fields is thine there,
open lies the land, yet the steely going
darkly hast thou dared and the dreaded aether
                parted before thee.

Swift at courage thou in the shell of gold, cast-
ing a-loose the cloak of the body, calmest
straight, then shone thine oriel and the stunned light
                faded about thee.

      – Ezra Pound, from "Apparent"

Exquisite torment, dainty Mrs. Hargreaves
Trips down the High Street, slaying hearts a-plenty;
Stricken and doomed are all who meet her eye-shots!
              Bar Mr. Hargreaves.

Grocers a-tremble bash their brassy scales down,
Careless of weight and hacking cheese regardless;
Postmen shoot letters in the nearest ashcan,
                              Dogs dance in circles.

Leaving their meters, gas-inspectors gallop,
Water Board men cease cutting off the water;
Florists are strewing inexpensive posies
                              In Beauty's pathway...

> —Timothy Shy (Wyndham Lewis), from *Wyndham*
> *Lewis: Collected Poems and Plays*

O you chorus of indolent reviewers,
Irresponsible, indolent reviewers,
Look, I come to the test, a tiny poem
All composed in a metre of Catullus,
All in quantity, careful of my motion,
Like the skater on ice that hardly bears him,
Lest I fall unawares before people,
Waking laughter in indolent reviewers.
Should I flounder awhile without a tumble
Thro' this metrification of Catullus,
They should speak to me not without a welcome,
All that chorus of indolent reviewers.
Hard, hard, hard is it, only not to bumble,
So fantastical is the dainty metre.

Wherefore slight me not wholly, nor believe me
Too presumptuous, indolent reviewers.
O blatant Magazines, regard me rather—
Since I blush to belaud myself a moment—
As some rare little rose, a piece of inmost
Horticultural art, or half coquette-like
Maiden, not to be greeted unbenignly.

> —Tennyson, from "Milton—Hendecasyllabics"

Cēnā | bīs běně: | nām tǔ | ī Cǎ | tūllǐ

> — Catullus (Hendecasyllabics), from *The Poems of Catullus*

Ádeste, | hēndĕcă|syllăb|ī, quŏt | ēstīs

> — Catullus (Hendecasyllabics), from *The Poems of Catullus*

Truest-hearted of early friends, that Eton
Long since gave to me,—Ah! 'tis all a life-time,—
With my faithfully festive auspication
Of Christmas merriment, this idle item…

If this be not a holy consolation
More than plumpudding and a turkey roasted,
Whereto you but address a third dimension,
Try it, pray, as a pill to aid digestion:
I can't find anything better to send you.

> — Robert Bridges, from "The Fourth Dimension"

O mighty-mouth'd inventor of harmonies,
O skill's to sing of Time or Eternity,
      God-gifted organ-voice of England,
          Milton, a name to resound for ages;…
Where some refulgent sunset of India
Streams o'er a rich ambrosial ocean isle,
      And crimson-hued the stately palm-woods
          Whisper in odorous heights of even.

> —Tennyson, from "Milton—Alcaics"

Now, while the west-wing slumbereth on the lake,
Silently dost thou with delicate shimmer
      O'erbloom the frowning front of awful
          Night to a glance of unearthly silver.

No hungry wild beast rangeth in our forest,
No tiger or wolf prowleth around the fold:
      Keep thou from our sheepcotes the tainting
          Invisible peril of the darkness.

> — Bridges, from *Poetical Works of Robert Bridges*

Let thy west wind sleep on
The lake: speak silence with thy glimmering eyes,
And wash the dusk with silver.—Soon, full soon,
Dost thou withdraw; then the wolf rages wide,
And then the lion glares through the dun forest.
The fleeces of our flocks are covered with
Thy sacred dew: protect them with thine influence!

— Blake, from "To the Evening Star"

It is possible in English to practice a purely quantitative system, so long as one adopts a set of rules for determining long and short syllables. But the result is extremely arbitrary and unsatisfactory. What does work rather better is to adopt the standard Greek or Latin metres, such as the hexameter, and change the longs and shorts into accents and unaccented syllables. In skilful hands the results are not devoid of interest, as Arthur Hugh Clough demonstrated in his *Amors de Voyage*:

Ah, for a child in the street I could strike; for the full-blown lady—

Somehow, Eustace, alas! I have not felt the vocation.

— J. McAuley, from *Versification*

MORE RENAISSANCE EXAMPLES

But above all the accent of our words is diligently to be observ'd, for chiefly by the accent in any language the true value of the syllables is to be measured. Neither can I remember any impediment except position that can alter the accent of any syllable in our English verse. For though we accent the second of *Trumpington* short, yet is it naturally long, and so of necessity must be held of every composer. Wherefore the first rule that is to be observed, is the nature of the accent, which we must ever follow.

The next rule is position, which makes every sillable long, whether the position happens in one or in two words, according to the manner of the *Latines*, wherein is to be noted that h is no letter.

Position is when a vowel comes before two consonants, either in one or two words. In one, as in *best*, *e* before *st*, makes the word *best* long by position. In two words, as in *settled love*: *e* before *d* in the last sillable of the first word, and *l* in the beginning of the second makes *led* in *settlēd* long by position.

A vowel before a vowel is always short, as, *flĭīng*, *dĭīng*, *gŏīng*, unlesse the accent alter it, as in *dĕnīing*.

The dipthong in the midst of a word is always long, as *plaīing*, *deceīving*.

The *Synalaephas* or *Elisions* in our toong are either necessary to avoid the owwnes and gaping in our verse as to, and the, *t'incaunt*, *th'inchaunter*, or may be used at pleasure, as for *let us*, to say *let's*, for *we will*, *wee'l*, for *every*, *ev'ry*, for *they are*, *th'ar*, for *he is*, *hee's*, for *admired*, *admir'd*, and such like....

In words of two syllables, if the last have a full and rising accent that sticks long upon the voice, the first sillable is always short, unlesse position, or the dipthong doth make it long, as *dĕsīre*, *prĕsērve*, *dĕfīne*, *prŏphāne*, *rĕgārd*, *mănūre*, and such like.....

Words of two syllables that in their last sillable mayntayne a flat or falling accent, ought to hold their first sillable long, as *rīgŏr, glōrĭes, spīrĭt, fŭrĭe, lăbŏŭr*, and the like: *ăny, măny, prĕtty, hŏly*, and their like, are expected.

One observation which leades me to judge of the difference of these disillables whereof I last spake, I take from the originall monasillable, which if it be grave, as *shāde*, I hold that the first of *shādĭe* must be long, so *trūe, trūlĭe, hāve, hāvĭng, tīre, tīrĭng*...

Re is ever short, as *rĕmĕdĭe, rĕvĕrēnce, rĕdŏlēnt, rĕvĕrēnd*...

All monasillables that end in a grave accent are ever long, as *wrāth, hāth, thēse, thōse, tōoth, sōoth, thrōugh, dāy, plāy, seāte, speēde, strīfe, slōw, grōw, shēw*...

These monasillables are always short, as *ă, thĕ, thĭ, shĕ, wĕ, bĕ, hĕ, nŏt, tŏ, gŏ, sŏ, dŏ*, and the like....

The last sillable of all words in the plural number that have two or more vowels before s, are long, as *vertūes, dutīes, miserīes, fellowēs*...

(Another kind consists of a *Dimeter* whose) first foote may either be a *Sponde* or a *Trochy*: the two verses following are bothe of them *Trochaical*, and consist of foure feete, the first of either of them being a *Sponde* or *Trochy*, the other three only *Trochyes*. The fourth and last verse is made of two *Trochyes*. The number is voluble and fit to expresse any amorous conceit.

The Example.

   Rose-cheekt Lawra come
Sing thous smoothly with thy beawties
Silent musick, either other
               Sweetely gracing.
     Lovely formes do flowe
From concent divinely framed,
Heav'n is musick, and they beawties
            Birth is heavenly.
    These dull notes we sing

Discords neede for helps to grace them,
Only beawty purely loving
                    Knowes no discord:
            But still mooves delight
Like cleare springs renu'd by flowing,
Ever perfet, ever in them—
                    selves eternall.

The English Sapphick.

…

Their plum'd pomp the vulgar heaps detaineth,
And rough steeds, let us the still devices
Close observe, the speeches and the musicks
                    Peacefull arms adorning.
But whence showres so fast this angry tempest,
Clouding dimme the place? Behold Eliza
This day shines not here, this heard, the launches
                    And thick heads do vanish.

—Thomas Campion, *Observations in the Art of English Poesies*

…

Yet dying, and dead, doo we sing her honor;   – ◡ – – – ◡ – ◡ – –
So become our tombes monuments of her praise;   – ◡ – – – ◡ – ◡ – –
So becomes our losse the triumph of her gayne;   – ◡ – – – ◡ – ◡ – –
            Hers be the glory.   – ◡ ◡ – –
If the sencelesse spheares doo yet hold a musique,
If the Swanne's sweet voice be not heard, but at death,
If the mute timber when it hath the life lost.   [Sidney's paradigm]

…

My muse what sils this ardour?
My eys be dym, my lyms shake,   ◡ – ◡ – ◡ – –
My voice is hoarse, my throte scorcht,   [*Anacreontic*,
My tong to this my roofer cleaves,   Sidney's paradigm]
My fancy amazed, my thoughts dull'd,
My harte doth ake, my life faints,
My sole beginners to take leave.

So greate a passion all feele,
To think a soare so deadly
I should so rashly ripp up.

. . .

O sweete woods the delight of solitarines!
O how much I do like your solitarines!
Here no treason is hidd, vailed in innocence,   – – – ᴗ ᴗ – – ᴗ ᴗ – ᴗ
Nor envie's snaky ey, finds any harbor here,   [*Asclepiadic,*
Nor flatterers' venomous insinuations,   Sidney's paradigm]
Nor conning humorists' puddled opinions,
Nor courteous ruin of proffered usury,
Nor time prattled away, cradle of ignorance,
Nor causelesse duty, nor comber of arrogance,
Nor trifling title of vanity dazzleth us,
Nor golden manacles, stand for a paradise,
Here wrong's name is unheard: slander a monster is.
Keeper thy sprite from abuse, here no abuse doth haunte.
What man grafts in a tree dissimulation?

. . .

Gladly my senses yielding,
Thus to betray my hart's fort,
Left me devoid of all life...

                                                    – ᴗ ᴗ – ᴗ – –

Thus do I fall to rise thus,   [*Aristophanic,*
Thus do I dye to live thus,   Sidney's paradigm]
Changed to a change, I change not.

Thus may I not be from you:
Thus be my senses on you:
Thus what I thinker is of you:
Thus what I seeker is in you:
    All what I am, it is you.

                    – Sidney, from Complete Poems of *Sir Philip Sidney*

PRACTICE EXERCISES

PART I.

Mark the scansion of this passage, using the sign ˘ for a weak or light syllable and the sign ′ for a strong or heavy syllable. Mark the end of each fact with a diagonal or slash:

Finally, note that one of the lines is not metrically correct (I have altered it): this line you should mark simply with an asterisk or arrow.

Rumble thy bellyful! Spit, fire! spout, rain!

Nor rain, wind, thunder, fire, are daughters:

I tax not you, you elements, with unkindness;

I never gave you kingdom, called you children,

You owe me no subscription: then let fall

Your horrible pleasure; here I stand, your slave,

A poor, infirm, weak and despised old man:

But yet I call you servile fellows,

That have with two pernicious daughters joined

Your high-engendered battles 'gainst a head

So old and white as this. O! O! 'tis foul!

— Shakespeare, from King Lear

PART II.

One passage below is prose; the others are in verse, printed here as prose. There is at least one example of each of the metrical types we have so far considered—syllabics, accentuals, and accentual-syllabics (this last category would, of course, include song meters). Here's what you should do:

1) For each passage, excepting the one in prose, which you should leave unmarked, simply indicate by means of diagonals (/) the divisions between lines, as in this example:

> For two years I looked forward only to breakfast. The
> night was not night, it was tempered by hotel signs
> opposite.

This process should reveal the type of meter used in each passage and, in some cases, other aspects of its form as well, such as rhyme and stanzaic structure, if any.

2) Now identify—that is, name, with one of our agreed-upon terms (syllabics, accentuals, accentual-syllabics)—the type of meter used in each passage and add any other clarifying or characterizing comments you might consider helpful, if any. (For example, the above passage beginning, "For two years," is in syllabics, the lines having 7 syllables each.)

> A. Sweet Kate of late ran away and left me paining. Abide I cried or I die with thy disdaining. Te he hee quote she gladly would I see any man to die with loving, never any yet died of such a fit: neither have I fear of proving. Unkind, I find thy delight is in tormenting, abide, I cried, or I die with thy consenting. Te he hee quoth she, make no fool of me, men I know have oaths at pleasure, but their hopes attained, they betray they feigned, and their oaths are kept at leisure. Her words like swords cut my sorry heart in sunder, her flouts, with doubts, kept my heart's

affections under. Te he hee quoth she, what a fool is he stands in awe of once denying, cause I had enough to become more rough, so I did, O happy trying.

— Jones, from "Sweet Kate"

Type:
Comments, if any:

B. The night is chill; the forest bare; it is the wind that month bleak? There is not wind enough in the air to move away the ringlet curl from the lovely lady's cheek—there is not wind enough to twirl the one red leaf, the last of its clan, that dances as often as dance it can, hanging so light, and hanging so high, on the topmost twig that looks up at the sky.

— Coleridge, from *Christabel*

Type:
Comments, if any:

C. We rode past a pier where freshly caught fish were being weighed. Their bizarre colors, gory skin wounds, glassy eyes, mouths full of congealed blood, sharp-pointed teeth– all were evidence of a wickedness as deep as the abyss. Men gutted the fishes with an unholy joy. The bus passed a snake farm, a monkey colony. I saw houses eaten up by termites and a pond of brackish water in which the descendants of the primeval snake crawled and slithered. Parrots screeched with strident voices. At times, strange smells blew in through the bus window, stenches so dense they made my head throb.

— Singer, from "Sammlung"

Type:
Comments, if any:

D. Your fly will serve as well as anybody, and what's his hour? He flies, and flies, and flies, and in his fly's mind has a brave appearance; and then your spider gets him in her net, and eats him out, and hangs him up to dry. That's Nature, the kind mother

of us all. And then your slattern housemaid swings her broom,
and where's your spider? And that's Nature also. It's Mature, and
it's Nothing. It's all Nothing.

— Robinson, from "Ben Jonson Entertains a Man from Stratford"

Type:
Comments, if any:

E. My Dear One is mine as mirrors are lonely, as the poor and
sad are real to the good king, and the high green hill sits always
by the sea. At his crossroads, too, the Ancient prayed for me;
down his wasted cheeks tears of joy were running: my Dear One
is mine as mirrors are lonely. He kissed me awake, and no one
was sorry; the sun shone on the sails, eyes, pebbles, anything,
and the high green hill sits always by the sea.

—Auden, from "Miranda"

Type:
Comments, if any:

PART III.

Fill in the blanks in the following passages from among the words given as
multiple choices. Further, in each passage one line is metrically incorrect: you
should identify that line by means of an asterisk or arrow.

A. Come, my Celia, let us prove,
While we can, the sports of love.
Time will not be ours for ever;   (1) everlasting
He, at length, our good will sever.   perpetual
Spend not then his rewards in vain: dark
Suns that set may rise again.   darksome
But if once we lose this light,
'Tis with us (1)_____ night.   (2) decoys
Why should we defer our joys?   words
Fame and rumor are but (2)_____.   toys
                                                 abstractions

B. Dürer would have seen a reason for living   (3) sharks
   In a town like this, with eight stranded (3)_____   females
to look at; with the sweet sea air coming into your house   nightingales
on a fine day, from water etched   whales
  with waves as formal as the scales   cows
on a fish.   snails
           (4) wings
One by one, in two's, in three's, the seagulls keep   underpinnings
  flying back and forth over the town clock,   feathers
or sailing around the lighthouse without moving their (4)_____

rising steadily with a slight   (5) hung
  quiver of the body—or flock   ranged
mewing where below them   arranged
         spread-out

a sea the purple of the peacock's neck is
  paled to a greenish azure of Durer changed
the pine green of the Tyrol to peacock blue and guinea
grey. You can see a twenty-five-
  pound lobster and fish-nets (5)_____
to dry.

EXERCISE FOR PERMISSIVE VARIATIONS

Indicate the scansion of the following lines, but do not concern yourself overmuch with subtleties & niceties. Use only a two-value stress system (that is, a given syllable will be—in these lines—either relatively weak or relatively strong). Allow yourself to hear and mark only the so-called "permissive" variations, for a weakly stressed syllable; for a strongly stressed syllable.

Example: Sunk though | he be | beneath | the wat | ery floor.

Or: Sunk though | he be | beneath | the wat | ery floor.

(You need not provide such alternative readings. I do so only to illustrate that there may be more than one correct marking.)

Back out of all this now too much for us,

Back in a time made simple by the loss

Of detail, burned, dissolved, and broken off

Like graveyard marble sculpture in the weather,

There is a house that is no more a house

Upon a farm that is no more a farm

And in a town that is no more a town.

The road there, if you'll let a guide direct you

Who only has at heart your getting lost,

May seem as if it should have been a quarry—

Great monolithic knees the former town

Long since gave up pretence of keeping covered.

And there's a story in a book about it:

Besides the wear of iron wagon wheels

The ledges show lines ruled southeast northwest,

The chisel work of an enormous Glacier

That braced his feet against the Arctic Pole.

You must not mind a certain coolness from him

Still said to haunt this side of Panther Mountain.

> — Frost, from "Directive"

FURTHER LINES TO MARK THE SCANSION OF:

(Don't bother to mark the divisions into feet.)

1. Let twenty pass, and stone the twenty-first,

Loving not, hating not, just choosing so.

2. Here had been, mark, the general-in-chief,

Thro' a whole campaign of the world's life and death,

Doing the King's work all the dim day long,

In his old coat and up to his knees in mud,

Smoked like a herring, dining on a crust.

3. Back I shrink—what is this I see and hear?

I, caught up with my monk's things by mistake,

My old serge gown and rope that goes all round,

I, in this presence, this pure company!

Where's a hole, where's a corner for escape?

4. Good strong thick stupefying incense-smoke!

5. 'Do I live, am I dead?' There, leave me, there!

6. And at their feet the crocus brake like fire,

Violet, amaracus and asphodel,

Lotus and lilies: and a wind arose,

And overhead the wandering ivy and vine,

This way and that, in many a wild festoon.

Ran riot, garlanding the gnarled boughs.

7. It may be nothing of a sort more noisy

Than a small oblivion of component ashes.

8. A reason for man's once having and leaving her.

9. Where the cold waves that rolled along the sand

Were saying to her unceasingly, "Tristram —

Tristram." She heard them and was unaware.

10. Hovered an air of still simplicity

And a fragrance of old summers—the old style

11. To you, and as you need it.——But there, there...

12. The quaint thin crack in Archibald's voice

13. "I've got you, Isaac; high, low, jack, and the game."

14. And in her eyes there was a flickering

Of a still fear that would not be veiled wholly.

15. See now, and shall see. There are no more lies.

16. Something came over me like the discovery

Of a deep secret of the universe.

It was dearly. I was in the dining room

Long before breakfast was served. I was alone.

17. "Sand grains should sugar in the natal dew

The babe born to the desert, the sand storm

Retard mid-waste my cowering caravans —

There are bees in this wall." He struck the clapboards,

Fierce heads looked out; small bodies pivoted.

We rose to go. Sunset blazed on the windows.

18. Complacencies of the peignoir, and late

Coffee and oranges in a sunny chair,

And the green freedom of a cockatoo...

19. It was almost time for lunch. Pain was human.

There were roses in the cool café. His book

Made sure of the most correct catastrophe.

Of the types of verse we considered, there should be found here at least 3 examples each of the following, not all of them quite pure or unmixed: (1) accentual-syllabics, (2) accentual, (3) syllabics, (4) long-line free verse (Psalmic or Whitmanesque), (5) long-line free verse (Websterea or loosened blank verse), (6) short-line free verse (Imagist or Stevens-like), & (7) short-line free verse (Williams-like). In addition, one passage does not fit into any of the above types.

Identify all examples as to type. (For the one that does not fit, just say that it does not, unless you care to go further.)

Then comment on & describe the meter of 1 passage of blank verse & of 1 other type of accentual-syllabics; & do the same for 1 passage belonging to each of the other types—in whatever way you believe is illuminating. This may or may not involve a little scansion. Do not overdo it or write too much.

> 1. By a route obscure and lonely,
> Haunted by ill angels only,
> Where an Eidolon, named NIGHT,
> On a black throne reigns upright,
> I have reached these lands but newly
> From an ultimate dim Thule –
> From a wild weird clime that lieth, sublime,
>   Out of SPACE—out of TIME.

> 2. This darksome burn, horseback brown,
> His rollrock highroad roaring down,
> In coop and in comb the fleece of his foam
> Flutes and low to the lake falls home.

A windpuff-bonnet of fawn-froth
Turns and dwindles over the broth
Of a pool so pitchblack, fell-frowning,
It rounds and rounds Despair to drowning.

Degged with dew, dappled with dew
Are the groins of the braes that the brook treads through,
Wiry heathpacks, fitches of fern,
And the beadbonny ash that sits over the burn.

What would the world be, once bereft
Of wet and of wilderness? Let them be left,
O let them be left, wildness and wet;
Long live the weeds and the wilderness yet.

3. Her sister, hearing of her imprisonment,
confronted the Bache
and begged to be made captive,
though innocent of Denise's crime.
Whatever their motive, they complied.
The Lord have mercy on her.

They came finally to the Natzweiler Camp,
where the sick were gassed,
and her sister being ill,
Denise begged to be chosen as well.
Thus, these daughters of France came to embrace Death.
The Lord have mercy on them.

4. The fog comes
on little cat feet.
It sits looking
over harbor and city
on silent haunches
and then moves on.

5. What if released in air
it became a white

source of light, a fountain
of light? Could all that weight

be the power of flight?
Look inward: see me

with embryo wings, one
feathered in soot, the other

blazing ciliations of ember, pale
flare-pinions. Well—

could I go
on one wing,

the white one?

6. Does Nun Snow,
Aware of the death she must die alone,
Away from the nuns
Of the green beads,
Of the ochre and brown,
Of the purple and black—
Does she improvise
Along those soundless strings
In the worldly hope
That the answering, friendly tune,
The faithful, folk-like miracle,
Will shine in a moment or two?

7. The iridescent vibrations of midsummer light
Dancing, dancing, suddenly flickering and quivering
Like little feet or the movement of quick hands clapping,
Or the rustle of furbelows or the clash of polished gems.
The palpitant mosaic of the midday light
Colliding, sliding, leaping and lingering:
O, I could lie on my back all day,
And mark the mad ballet of the midsummer sky.

8. So we moved, and they, in a formal pattern,
Along the empty alley, into the box circle,
To look down into the drained pool.
Dry the pool, dry concrete, brown edged,
And the pool was filled with water out of sunlight,
And the lotos rose, quietly, quietly,
And they were behind us, reflected in the pool.
Then a cloud passed, and the pool was empty.

9. When I saw the woman's leg on the floor of the subway train,
Protrude beyond the panel (while her body overflowed my mind's eye),
When I saw the pink stocking, black shoe, curve bulging with warmth,
The delicate etching of the hair behind the flesh-colored gauze,
When I saw the ankle of Mrs. Nobody going nowhere for a nickel,
When I saw this foot motionless on the moving motionless floor,
My mind caught on a nail of a distant star, I was wrenched out
Of the reality of the subway ride, I hung in a socket of distance.

10. I write. My mother was a Florentine,
Whose rare blue eyes were shut from seeing me
When scarcely I was four years old, my life
A poor spark snatched up from a failing lamp
Which went out therefore. She was weak and frail;
She could not bear the joy of giving life,
The mother's rapture slew her. If her kiss
Had left a long weight upon my lips
It might have steadied the uneasy breath.

11. These retroactive
instances of feeling
reach out for a common
ground in the wet

first rain of a faded
winter. Along the grey

iced sidewalk revealed
piles of dogshit, papers,

bits of old clothing, are
the human pledges,

call them, "We are here and
have been all the time." I

walk quickly. The wind
drives the rain, drenching

my coat, pants, blurs
my glasses, as I pass.

12. These are the facts. The uncle, the elder brother, the squire (a
Little embarrassed, I fancy), resides in a family place in
Cornwall, of course; 'Papa is in business,' Mary informs me;
He's a good sensible man, whatever his trade is. The mother
Is—shall I call it fine?—herself she would tell you refined, and
Greatly, I fear me, looks down on my bookish and maladroit manners;
Somewhat affecteth the blue; would talk to me often of poets;
Quotes, which I hate, Childe Harold; but also appreciates
Wordsworth.

13. The wind turned
me round and
round all day, so
cold it planed
me, quick it

polished me
down: a spindle
by dusk,
too lean to
bear the open dark,

I said, sky,
drive me
into the
ground here,
still me with the ground.

14. Just now,
Out of the strange
Still dusk… as strange, as still…
A white moth flew. Why am I grown
So cold?

15. The light is like a spider.
It crawls over the water.
It crawls over the edges of the snow.
It crawls under your eyelids
And spreads its webs there—
Its two webs.

The web of your eyes
Are fastened
To the flesh and bones of you
As to rafters or grass.

16. O wind, rend open the heat,
Cut apart the heat,
Slit it to tatters.

Fruit cannot drop
Through this thick air;
Fruit cannot fall into heat
That presses up and blunts
The points of pears,
And rounds the grapes.

Cut the heat:
Plough through it,
Turning it on either side
Of your path.

17. Underneath this pretty cover
Lies Vanessa, Stella's lover.
You that undertake this story
For his life nor death be sorry

Who the Absolute so moved,
Till immobile in that chill
Fury hardened in the will,
And the trivial, bestial flesh
In its jacket ceased to thresh,
And the soul none dare forgive
Quiet lay, and ceased to live.

18. There's a certain Slant of light,
Winter afternoons—
That oppresses, like the Heft
Of Cathedral Tunes—

When it comes, the Landscape listens—
Shadows—hold their breath—
When it goes, 'tis like the Distance
On the look of Death—

19. Drum on your drums, batter on your banjos, sob on the
long cool winding saxophones. Go to it, O jazzmen.

   Sling your knuckles on the bottoms of the happy tin pans,
let your trombones ooze, and go husha-husha-hush with the
slippery sandpaper.

   Moan like an autumn wind high in the lonesome treetops,
moan soft like you wanted something terrible, cry like a
racing car slipping away from a motorcycle-cop, bang-bank!
you jazzmen, bang altogether drums, traps, banjos, horns,
tin cans—make two people fight on the top of a stairway and
scratch each other's eyes in a clinch tumbling down the stairs.

20. The horns in the harbor booming, vaguely,
Fog, forgotten, yesterday, conclusion,
Nostalgic, noising dim sorrow, calling
To sleep is it? I think so, and childhood,

Not the door opened and the stair descended,
The voice answered, the choice announced,
Trigger touched in sharp declaration!

And when it comes, escape is small; the door
Creaks; the worms of fear spread veins; the furtive
Fugitive, looking backward, sees his
Ghost in the mirror, his shameful eyes, his mouth diseased.

21. Hasbrouck was there and so were Bill
And Smollet Smith the poet, and Ames was there.
After his thirteenth drink, the burning Smith,
Raising his fourteenth trembling in the air,
Said, "Drink with me, Bill, drink up to the Rose."
But Hasbrouck laughed like old men in a myth,
Inquiring, "Smollet, are you drunk? What rose?"
And Smollet said, "I drunk? It may be so;
Which comes from brooding on the flower, the flower
I mean toward which mad hour by hour
I travel brokenly; and I shall know,
With Hermes and the alchemists—but, hell,
What use is it talking that way to you?
Hard-boiled, unbroken egg, what can you care
For the enfolded passion of the Rose?"

22. Buffaloes, buffaloes, thousands abreast,
A scourge and amazement, they swept to the west.
With black bobbing noses, with red rolling tongues,
Coughing forth steam from their leather –wrapped lungs,
Cows with their calves, bulls big and vain,
Goring the laggards, shaking the mane,
Stamping flint feet, flashing moon eyes,
Pompous and owlish, shaggy and wise.

23. In the desert
I saw a creature, naked, bestial,

Who, squatting upon the ground,
Held his heart in his hands,
And ate of it.

I said, "Is it good, friend?"
"It is bitter—bitter," he answered,
"But I like it
Because it is bitter,
And because it is my heart."

24. There were three sisters fair and bright,
Jennifer gentle and rosemaree,
And they three loved one valiant knight.
As the dew flies over the mulberry tree.

The eldest sister let him in,
And barred the door with a silver pin.
The second sister made his bed,
And placed soft pillows under his head.

The youngest sister, fair and bright,
Was resolved for to wed with this valiant knight.

25. All
external
     marks of abuse are present on this
     defiant edifice—
        all the physical features of

ac-
cident—lack
     of cornice, dynamite grooves, burns, and
     hatchet strokes, these things stand
        out on it; the chasm-side is

dead.
Repeated

evidence has proved that it can live
on what can not revive
    its youth. The sea grows old in it.

26. Love and forgetting might have carried them
A little further up the mountain side
With night so near, but not much further up.
They must have halted soon in any case
With thoughts of the path back, how rough it was
With rock and washout, and unsafe in darkness;
When they were halted by a tumbled wall
With barbed-wire binding. They stood facing this,
Spending what onward impulse they still had
In one last look the way they must not go.

27. At the equinox when the earth was veiled in a late rain, wreathed
    with wet poppies, waiting spring,
The ocean swelled for a far storm and beat its boundary, the ground
    swell shook the beds of granite.

I gazing at the boundaries of granite and spray, the established sea
    marks, felt behind me
Mountain and plain, the immense breadth of the continent, before me
    the mass and doubled stretch of water.

I said: You yoke the Aleutian seal-rocks with the lava and coral sowings
    that flower the south,
Over your flood the life that sought the sunrise faces ours that has
    followed the evening star.

A SELECTIVE BIBLIOGRAPHY

Allen, Donald & Tallman, Warren, eds., THE POETICS OF THE NEW AMERICAN POETRY, Grove Press, 1973.

Auden, W.H., Kallman, Chester, & Greenberg, Noah, eds., AN ELIZABETHAN SONG BOOK, Doubleday, 1955.

Berdan, J.M., EARLY TUDOR POETRY, 1920.

Blake, William, "Of the Measure in Which Jerusalem Is Written," c. 1820.

Bridges, Robert, MILTON'S PROSODY, Oxford, 1901.

Campion, Thomas, OBSERVATIONS IN THE ART OF ENGLISH POESIE, 1602.

Coleridge, Samuel Taylor, "Preface to Cristobel," 1816.

Cunningham, J.V., THE COLLECTED ESSAYS OF J.V. CUNNINGHAM, Swallow Press, 1976.

Eliot, T.S., TO CRITICIZE THE CRITIC, Farrar Straus, 1965.

Fussell, Paul, POETIC METER AND POETIC FORM, 1979, revised edition.

Gross, Harvey, SOUND AND FORM IN MODERN POETRY, University of Michigan Press, 1965.

Hemphill, George, ed., DISCUSSIONS OF POETRY: RHYTHM AND SOUND, D.C. Heath, 1961. (Contains, among many other interesting items, the early KENYON REVIEW symposium on linguistics and prosody.)

Hollander, John, RHYME'S REASON: A GUIDE TO ENGLISH VERSE, Yale University Press, 1981.

Hope, A.D., "Free Verse: A Post Mortem," Quadrant (Australia), IV, 1, 1960.

Hopkins, G.M., "Author's Preface" in THE POEMS OF GERARD MANLEY HOPKINS, Oxford, 1967.

Jones, P. Mansell, THE BACKGROUND OF MODERN FRENCH POETRY, Cambridge, 1951.

Justice, Donald, PLATONIC SCRIPTS, University of Michigan Press, 1984.

Kahn, Gustave, ed. Vogue, 1886. (Periodical)

Lowell, Robert, The Paris Review, #25, pp. 56-95 (no date given).

MaCauley, James, VERSIFICATION: A SHORT INTRODUCTION, Michigan State University Press, 1966.

Nabolov, Vladimir, transl., EUGENE ONEGIN, III, Appendix 2, pp. 452-4.

Pace, George B., "The Two Domains: Meter and Rhythm," PMLA, LXXVI, 4, part 1, pp. 413-9.

Pike, Kenneth L., THE INTONATION OF AMERICAN ENGLISH, University of Michigan Press, 1945.

Pound, Ezra, THE LITERARY ESSAYS OF EZRA POUND, New Directions, 1954.

Preminger, Alex, Warnke, F.J., & Hardison, O.B., Jr., PRINCETON ENCYCLOPEDIA OF POETRY AND POETICS, Princeton University Press, 1974, enlarged edition.

Ransom, John Crowe, BEATING THE BUSHES, New Directions, 1972 (for "Wanted: An Ontological Critic").

Ransom, John Crowe, THE WORLD'S BODY, Scribner's, 1938.

Ringler, W.A., ed., THE POEMS OF SIR PHILIP SIDNEY, Oxford, 1962, p. 391 ff.

Saintsbury, George, A HISTORY OF ENGLISH PROSODY, Macmillan, 1906-10.

Thompson, John, THE FOUNDING OF ENGLISH METRE, Columbia, 1966.

Williams, W.C., SELECTED LETTERS, New Directions, 1957.

Wimsatt, W.K., & Beardsley, Monroe, "The Concept of Meter: An Exercise in Abstraction," PMLA, LXXIV, pp. 585-98.

Wordsworth, William, "Poetry and Poetic Diction (Preface to the Second Edition of LYRICAL BALADS), 1800.

ADDENDA

Barzun, Essay on French Verse, New Directions Press.

O.B. Hardisch, Prosody and Purpose in the English Renaissance, John Hopkins Press 1989.

Derrek Attridge, Rhythms of English Poetry, Longman 1982.

FOR THE WORKBOOK MODULES

To download the supplemental Workbook Modules created by David Koehn and Alan Soldofsky:

1. Visit www.omnidawn.com/prosody-workbook

2. Click the Download button

INDEX

Donald Justice delighted in the constraint of poetic form and the subtleties of meter, often finding his subjects in an unsentimental nostalgia for the past, and particularly for the South during the Great Depression. He cast a cool eye on the fashion of the moment—if there were rules, he loved to break them. Despite his reputation as a formal poet, Justice at times wrote poems using chance methods, once inventing a card game that could create a poem's syntax and vocabulary. A student of Robert Lowell, John Berryman, and Karl Shapiro at the Iowa Writers' Workshop, Justice became the most influential teacher in the history of the Iowa program, not just in the quiet attentions of the workshop but in the example of his poetry. His students at Iowa, and later at the University of Florida, included Mark Strand, Charles Wright, Jorie Graham, James Tate, Rita Dove, Lewis Turco, Norman Dubie, Larry Levis, Michael Ryan, Debora Greger, William Logan, Joe Bolton, and Geoffrey Brock. Justice was elected a chancellor of the Academy of American Poets and was offered the position of poet laureate, declining only because of ill health. His books of poetry included *The Summer Anniversaries* (1960), *Night Light* (1967), *Departures* (1973), *Selected Poems* (1979), *The Sunset Maker* (1987), *New and Selected Poems* (1995), and *Collected Poems* (2004). His criticism was collected in *Platonic Scripts* (1984) and *Oblivion* (1998). He received the Lamont Award, the Bollingen Prize, and the Pulitzer Prize.

Compendium: A collection of thoughts on Prosody
by Donald Justice
edited by David Koehn & Alan Soldofsky

Cover photo of Donald Justice courtesy of Barbara Hall, 1971

Cover and interior text set in Futura Std and Perpetua Std

Cover and interior design by Gillian Olivia Blythe Hamel

Offset printed in the United States
by Edwards Brothers Malloy, Ann Arbor, Michigan
On 55# Enviro Natural 100% Recycled 100% PCW
Acid Free Archival Quality FSC Certified Paper

Publication of this book was made possible in part by gifts from:
The New Place Fund
Robin & Curt Caton

Omnidawn Publishing
Oakland, California
2017

Rusty Morrison & Ken Keegan, senior editors & co-publishers
Gillian Olivia Blythe Hamel, managing editor
Cassandra Smith, poetry editor & book designer
Sharon Zetter, poetry editor, book designer & development officer
Liza Flum, poetry editor & marketing assistant
Peter Burghardt, poetry editor
Juliana Paslay, fiction editor
Gail Aronson, fiction editor
Cameron Stuart, marketing assistant
Avren Keating, administrative assistant
Kevin Peters, *OmniVerse* Lit Scene editor
Sara Burant, *OmniVerse* reviews editor
Josie Gallup, publicity assistant
SD Sumner, copyeditor
Briana Swain, marketing assistant